Your
Customer
Compass™

A Leader's Guide to Solid
Multi-Directional Business Success

SOLID EXECUTIVE COACHING, ADVISING, & CERTIFICATION | *Daniel J. Mueller*

Printed in the United States of America

First printing, 2021

ISBN 978-1-7352340-2-1

SOLIDleaders, LLC, 7301 FM 620 N Suite 155277 Austin, TX 78726

SOLIDleaders.com

Table of Contents

Acknowledgements

A special thanks to the Service Delivery Extended Leadership Team of Q2 Software for inspiring this work. Without you, this idea would still be rattling around inside my head. Because of you, and the annual offsites we do together, it is now on paper. I so appreciate all of you and look forward to future opportunities to work together.

To my staff at SOLID, thank you! Without you, I could not do what I do, and books like this would never come to fruition.

To those newly acquainted with SOLID, welcome! I hope the customer compass concept helps you and your team. May you enjoy reading this book as much as I have enjoyed writing it.

To all leaders, my this be one more powerful tool you use in your journey toward greater success.

—Daniel

Foreword

Like points on a compass, leaders have stakeholders in every direction. The board of directors, the management team, peers and teams from other functional areas, delivering a great customer experience requires close alignment amongst all these key constituents.

One of the major breakthroughs on one's journey to senior leadership is the recognition that the focus and discipline that is brought to serving customers needs to be brought to managing internal constituents as well, i.e. the customers from all vectors.

Executive coach Daniel Mueller has written a book that helps leaders at all levels to better deal with customers from all vectors. "Your Customer Compass" is a navigation tool to help you as you travel to the next level as a leader. The path to leadership excellence is difficult for many reasons, one of which is the large number of stakeholder bridges you need to build. If you construct your bridges successfully, two-way traffic flows easily, and clear communication and cooperation abounds.

I believe this book will give you helpful ideas on how to grow yourself and your team to be more effective bridge-builders as you construct effective pathways to the north, south, east and west, and be a valuable tool on your leadership journey.

Bharath Oruganti
Senior Vice President
Q2 Software
March 17, 2021

INTRODUCTION

Introduction

How well do you know your customers? The better you know them, the more likely you will succeed at making them happy. Happy customers usually mean thriving business. And thriving business usually means prosperity for all. So, customer satisfaction is often the key to a more prosperous future for you, personally and professionally.

The subtitle of this book speaks to our focus: *A Leader's Guide to Solid Multi-Directional Business Success.* There are four main directions in which you must excel as a leader. Many leaders are only successful in one or two directions, and ultimately do not succeed in growing their leadership careers.

It is critical to be successful in all four of the directions identified in *Your Customer Compass*. You can better do this if you have your bearings. That is what a compass is for.

But what if you have a misconception of who your customers are and what they want? What if you have biases that are throwing off your customer compass, much like a magnetic field will throw off a magnetometer compass?

Will that have a negative impact on you? Most assuredly.

In *Your Customer Compass*, you will explore key questions, including:

Who is my customer?
What do they want?
How can I best make them happy?
What is in it for me?

That last question is the most important. Back when I first started out as an organizational development consultant providing customer service training in the eighties, I heard it put like this: "The most listened-to radio station in the world is WIII FM. Everyone tunes in to it, no matter what they are doing. What Is In It For Me." I learned early on that if you want people to change their paradigm, expand their thinking, or go in a new direction, you need to give them the WIII FM.

So, let me tell you what is in it for you.

By grasping the following information, you will be guaranteed to:

1. Have a better career, getting promoted faster and more frequently, no matter what your level.

2. Earn greater compensation.

3. Be, and be seen as, a more valuable resource to everyone in your organization.

4. Become a better and more effective leader.

Are these extravagant promises? I think not. They will materialize for you, sometimes quickly, sometimes slowly, if you fully embrace the concepts found in this rapid-read book. You are likely already good at building bridges with certain stakeholders, and chances are, you are especially strong in one or two of the vectors we are about to discuss. Equally likely, one of these four areas will be your weakest. You probably over-index on one vector as well. And a strength overused becomes a weakness.

This is an opportunity to take a hard look at your strengths and weaknesses in building bridges with stakeholders. Where do you excel? Where are you weak? What will you do to become more successful at multi-directional business leadership?

What's in Your Pocket?

I love the Capital One commercial: "What's in your wallet?" Well, I have a similar question. Try to hear it in the same deep bass voice of the Capital One announcer.

What's in your pocket?

Figuratively speaking, in the pocket of every leader is a customer compass. It is a critical tool necessary for you to successfully navigate the often difficult and uncharted terrain of leadership. You are out in front, setting the course for your organization, identifying critical customers to serve and ensuring such service takes place.

In the literal sense, a compass helps you know the direction in which you are moving. This is called a **heading**. In business, we call that a **vision**. A compass helps you align or orient your map with your surroundings, which is called **setting the map**. In business, we call that our **strategic plan**. A compass also helps you work out the direction in which you will need to travel to reach an object or destination—its **bearing**. I call that your **customer**.

Quite frequently, you need to reach into your pocket, pull out your compass, and choose a direction.

You have stakeholders from the north, south, east and west all placing demands on your time and resources.

Where do you turn? Whom do you serve?

It is never easy and is always a balancing act.

As my good friend Joel Trammell, author of *The CEO Tightrope*, writes:

> *The CEO walks a tightrope daily, many times blindfolded and without a net below. The job of balancing the often-competing interests of a company's constituents is*

so challenging that the average lifespan of a newly minted CEO is around five years. Why is it that our most successful business-people, individuals who have been wildly successful at every other position in their career, often fail when they get to the CEO chair?[1]

I would go one step further and say that all leaders are walking the same tightrope. By my calculations, after conducting extensive research, the failure rate for director- and VP-level leaders starting a new role is between 19 and 21%, meaning one out of five get fired or quit in their first year. Why is that?

In addition, the "Peter Principle" is alive and well for those who have successfully grown and been promoted.

The "Peter Principle" is a concept in management developed by Laurence J. Peter, which observes that people in a hierarchy tend to rise to their "level of incompetence": employees are promoted based on their success in previous jobs until they reach a level at which they are no longer competent, as skills in one job do not necessarily translate to another.

The concept was explained in the book *The Peter Principle* (William Morrow and Company, 1969) by Dr. Peter and Raymond Hull:

The Peter Principle states that a person who is competent at their job will earn a promotion to a position that requires different skills. If the promoted person lacks the skills required for the new role, they will be incompetent at the new level, and will not be promoted again. If the person is competent in the new role, they will be promoted again and will continue to be promoted until reaching a level at which they are incompetent. Being incompetent, the individual will not qualify for promotion again, and so will remain stuck at this "Final Placement" or "Peter's Plateau."

---

1 Joel Trammell, *The CEO Tightrope: How to Master the Balancing Act of a Successful CEO* (Austin, Texas: Greenleaf Book Group Press, 2014)

This outcome is inevitable, given enough time and enough positions in the hierarchy to which competent employees may be promoted. The "Peter Principle" is therefore expressed as follows: "In a hierarchy, every employee tends to rise to his level of incompetence." This leads to Peter's Corollary: "In time, every post tends to be occupied by an employee who is incompetent to carry out its duties."[2]

As a leader, you walk a tightrope, balancing many competing demands. Edicts from the north. Crisis from the east. Sabotage from the west. Insurrection from the south. It sounds like a brutal battle, and it sometimes is, especially in cultures where leaders don't realize there are four distinct vectors on their customer compass, or never pull out this valuable tool and think directionally about whom they are serving and how. This is not the case with you, right now, here today.

---

2 "Peter Principle," Wikipedia, Wikimedia Foundation, Inc., last modified February 5, 2021, https://en.wikipedia.org/wiki/Peter_principle.

You want to serve the needs of all four vectors, but it is difficult. Looking down at a compass is really complicated when you are high above the ground without a net.

Come off your high-wire act for a little while, take a breath, and let's look at how it is possible for you to effectively address all four vectors equally well. You can do it. I know you can. It takes intentionality and determination. You can muster those. And it takes some reflection time. You deserve and need that time to get perspective.

Frenzied Activity Can Get You Quickly in the Wrong Direction

I got in my car and headed toward the highway home to Austin after an all-day client meeting in Houston. As is my custom, I jumped on the phone for back-to-back calls, making the three-hour drive more bearable and my time more productive. On the dashboard was a handy compass that showed my directional heading, which I ignored. After all, there were plenty of road signs indicating direction. Who needs a compass?

I quickly became engrossed in a deep conversation and ceased paying attention to road signs. As I found the I45 highway, I hit the gas. Flying down the road toward home. I could feel my bed.

An hour later, I hung up the phone and was ready for the next call when I realized that I must have missed the exit toward Austin. I had been driving on this road too long, and nothing looked familiar. By all accounts, I should have been in the middle of Houston. I got very confused because I was in thew middle of nowhere. How could this be? I glanced up at my compass. East! I was going east!

No way.

I was flying down the road, making excellent time, in the exact wrong direction. I had just added two hours to my three-hour drive. Expletives deleted. Ouch!

Sometimes I am so focused on maximum efficiency and getting things done that I lose sight of what is really important. Don Stoops, President of Cypress Semiconductor, taught me these two key sayings worth remembering as I worked with him in the late nineties:

"Humility is power, under control."

And,

"Sometimes you have to slow down in order to speed up."

That day, I "knew" where I was going and did not need help from any compass, or even road signs. My ego reveled at the sound of my engine kicking into high gear, flying down the highway. Speed. Power. It was exhilarating.

It never occurred to me to stop and check to make sure the end result of my effort was going to produce the desired outcome. Slowing down? Not a chance. I had things under control!

The message here is that it takes a great degree of humility to see your stakeholders as customers. And it takes discipline and intentionality to reflect on your customer compass, take inventory of the quality of your service to your stakeholders, and take corrective action where needed.

My premise is that you already have a working customer compass. My job is to bring your attention to it, help you use it, and show you how to do some mental navigation with it. Ultimately, by embracing the concepts here, you will get down the road faster, and be sure you are headed in the right direction.

My goals for this book are to:

1. Help you realize that you have a customer compass, that it is already in your pocket or on your dashboard, and that you can use it anytime you like.

2. Better define your customers in terms of four vectors: north, south, east, and west.

3. Equip you to walk this proverbial tightrope, go beyond surviving, and move into thriving as you grow your leadership to the next level of effectiveness.

4. Prevent you from becoming a victim of the "Peter Principle."

5. Provide a rapid read that can be easily assimilated in less than two hours.

To keep this more interesting, I have brought in some great authors who express their points much more eloquently than I can. They will greatly increase your spatial awareness, and I highly recommend these books to you for further exploration of the topics we will cover. I suggest you study the ones in the vector in which you are weakest.

And now, let's check our dashboard, check our compasses, and head north.

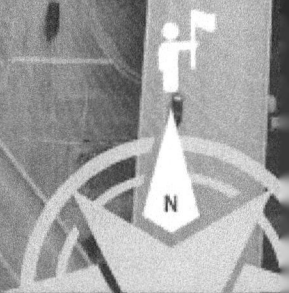

CHAPTER 1
NORTH

N

Chapter 1: NORTH

Art sat quietly in the back of the room. Always well dressed, this tall, slender, middle-aged entrepreneur looked quite distinguished with his trim beard. You could tell he was thinking as he was stroking his chin, likely wondering what on earth he had gotten himself into.

I, then a thirty-year-old consultant, was ten rows in front of him at the giant whiteboard, drawing out the Felco Office System Organizational Chart in front of Art's entire company. The first question made him squirm.

"Who is the most important person in this company?" I asked.

"Art," was the dutiful reply by a number of his loyal staff. They knew this was the right answer, and if anyone had any doubt, Art would remind them. Not only that, but hundreds of employees depended on Art, for he had made sure he was central to every department in the company. Art was the glue that held it all together, and he liked it that way.

Despite Art's best efforts to be everywhere at all times, he couldn't keep up with his growing company. That was why he'd hired me. He knew that things had to change for the company to continue to expand and had asked me and my organizational design and development consultancy to fix it. "Daniel," he had said, "I want this place to be less dependent on me. I want my people to take more initiative, and not wait for me to lead them into the right actions."

Leaders frequently have this dual pull. On the one hand, they want an empowered workforce like the one Art was demanding. On the other hand, they want to remain very much in control. They fear letting go of too much and losing a grip on performance, accountability, and authority. There I was, drawing out the organizational chart, about to discover one of the most transformational concepts of my career. I was clueless as to what was about to happen. I was just trying to demonstrate that this was a very complex organization and that one person at the top could not know all there was to know about every facet of the company. But transformation was right around the corner, and no one, least of all me, had any idea a breakthrough was about to occur.

Before I tell you what happened, allow me to give you a little insight into the professions of organizational development (OD) and executive coaching. Both deal with change management. OD is dealing with macro-level change on a company-wide or department-wide basis, whereas executive coaching is facilitating positive change on an individual level. Both help a person or a group "go to the next level of effectiveness." What you are about to see is an example of OD, followed by an example of executive coaching. My premise is that you need to be well versed in both disciplines and do your own OD of your organization and coaching of your direct reports.

"Who is the next most important set of people at Felco?" I probed. We quickly listed Art's senior vice presidents of Sales, Service, Accounting, HR, and Operations.

"Who's next?" I queried.

After a traditional organizational chart emerged, I said, "Well, it looks like we have accounted for all departments and functions. Good work." Nonchalantly, I asked, "Have we left anyone out?"

Some wise guy from the back of the room yelled, "The customer!"

"OK," I said, embracing the improvisational moment. I drew a long oblong box horizontally along the bottom of the org chart and labeled it "Customers." Then, it hit me. In a moment of sheer divine inspiration, I said, "Well, we thought of the customer last, so I guess they are not so important. So, we can erase them." I quickly erased the customer.

What happened next began the transformation of this company into a high-performance, customer-driven team. Art exclaimed, "If they go away, we go away!"

Following Art's lead, I enthusiastically erased the last half-hour of painstaking work we did drawing out Art's pyramid of a kingdom. I said, "Let's draw this out in order of what Art sees as important."

I redrew the Customer box across the entire top of the whiteboard and instantly knew where Art was going to end up. Sure enough, the team decided the next most important groups to depict were sales and service, because they had the most contact with the customer. After a number of layers, we finally got to Art's direct reports. And last but not least, Art, who was now at the very bottom of this inverted pyramid.

I called out to Art, "How does it feel to work your whole career just to end up at the bottom?"

"Great!" he exclaimed. "This is what has been missing here at Felco, a focus on the customer. I want this place to run well without me, and our customers to get well served, even when I am not around."

After this session, Art and I sat down in his office for a coaching session.

"Art, what did you think of today's session?" I asked.

"Interesting," he replied. "I am not sure if people really grasped all that you were saying."

"Art, what can you do to make sure this learning is really reinforced and becomes intrinsic change inside of Felco?"

"Great question. Let me think out loud for a minute."

An hour later, Art had a robust action plan that he faithfully implemented. It revolutionized his company and his life. Art was so happy with the outcome, he traded me his baby-blue Mercedes 380SL ragtop at below wholesale value in exchange for a year of additional work, making this one of my most memorable engagements ever.

Since that cold January day in 1987, I have recreated this same exercise thousands of times. And even though the inverted organizational chart is now known in many circles and used by numerous consultants I trained, and otherwise, the reaction I get from the head of an organization never ceases to amaze me. Instead of being taken aback at being deposed from their rightful place, they are more than willing to end up on the bottom of the pile if it means the external customer is elevated to the top.

Such is the case in your organization. Your leadership believe that external customers are the lifeblood of your company. Otherwise, I would not be here, and you would not be reading this. They want to embrace this "inverted organizational chart" idea and put the customer first. At the same time, they realize that they have other stakeholders they need to serve. They are actually pulled in four different directions, and so are you.

Let's look at these vectors and discuss them in terms of points on a compass: north, south, east and west. As we explore these quadrants, keep in mind that every leader has these same four sets of stakeholders, and ignoring one area can completely derail an organization and your career. However, what is more likely is that one vector is simply underserved. Together, we'll look at your customer compass and see how you may best serve each of your constituents.

Before we go there, however, I want to introduce the first of several leadership models that will help you think of all four vectors at once. Art had only been looking at one vector, the external customer to the east. Art was still Art, and still wanted to be served like a king.

He was still a top-down manager who did not listen to his people as well as he could have, had he taken the time and interest. It was still Art's way or the highway. Art's customers to the east benefited greatly by the transformation at Felco. However, Art had limited success with the business, and was plagued by challenges that could have been fixed if he had fully adopted the implications of his inverted organizational chart. One model that would have helped him is called *servant leadership*.

Servant Leadership

The best executives I know are naturally servant leaders, whether they know about this model or not. They don't want to be a king or queen served by others. They certainly don't want to be dictators. Most are enlightened nowadays to the critical need for employee empowerment. So, as you look north, you should see those who genuinely want to serve and support you as you in turn serve and support others. But how about you? Do you see your leader as someone you should serve? Do you see your role as making his or her work easier? When you look north, do you see that person you report to as a customer? Well, I believe they are. If you asked me to put your job description into the fewest possible words, I would say, "Your job is to make your leader's job easier."

In short, we can say that those to your north are your primary customers. To some, this may sound like heresy. "What about our REAL customer?" you may exclaim. "You know, the one that pays us—what about them?" My answer is simple. If you don't do a great job of meeting the needs of your primary customer, your leader, you will not be around to serve the ones you think are paying the bills. The following true story illustrates this fact.

When All You Want Is to Be Served

In 2002, I was providing executive coaching to Eileen Kamerick, CFO of one of the world's largest and still most successful executive search firms, Heidrick and Struggles. Eileen had recently hired a VP of Finance, Kevin, who was incredibly talented. He was extremely smart and very accomplished with an impeccable track record and impressive educational background. Kevin was a rock star.

There was only one problem. He was driving Eileen crazy. He was constantly causing upset on the team with all the changes he wanted to make. Admittedly, there were areas that needed improvement in Eileen's organization, but the way Kevin was going about it was causing so much noise that all Eileen could hear was the sound of breaking glass.

I came in and did an interview-based 360-degree assessment on Kevin, and the problem became crystal clear. Kevin did not listen. He did not have a customer compass. Consequently, his focus was serving everyone BUT Eileen. He was particularly fixated on the shareholders. Those were the stakeholders everyone was there to serve, right? I mean, if they didn't get the books closed on time, they were failing their stakeholders. So, Kevin did an awesome job of driving the entire Accounting and Finance organization to speed up the quarterly close, which they ended up doing in record time.

Looking west, his peers were in awe. "Great job, Kevin!" many exclaimed. But to his direct north, Eileen was miserable, because she was constantly fielding complaints from the south on how pushy Kevin was.

I delivered the 360-degree assessment report and facilitated a number of meetings where Kevin got to hear the negative impact he was having on his team to the south and on his leader, Eileen, but to no avail. Kevin just could not wrap his mind around the idea that Eileen and his directors were key customers he had to serve with the same passion he had for the shareholders. You can guess what happened next. He was let go a few months later, still puzzled as to what went wrong.

A strength overused becomes a weakness. Over-indexing on any one vector is guaranteed to cause problems in other vectors. Kevin's east-west highway was very well developed. His bridges with the street (Wall Street) and with peers were exceptional. He was an east-west kind of guy. I have seen many in my time as an external change agent. They don't last, or if they do, it is a mistake. This reminds me of a saying: "If the only tool you have is a hammer, every problem looks like a nail."

Well, if the only points on your compass are east-west, you are running in circles, missing two key stakeholder groups that will definitely make or break you. As an aside, this is why 360-degree feedback is so valuable. If you are over-indexing on serving one group, and under-indexing on serving another, often this assessment will point that out. It all comes back to age-old wisdom: "Be balanced." Running to extremes will cause magnetic interference and skew your compass readings.

Your Primary Job

For the next fifteen years I had the privilege of coaching Eileen through a number of major public-company CFO roles, and I learned more from her than she ever learned from me. The most critical thing she taught me was this idea that **a direct report's primary job is to make their leader's job easier**. This begs the question: Do you see this as your primary job? Can it be said that you are someone who makes your leader's job easier? Do you see your leader as a customer of yours? When you look north, how many customers do you see? How well are you serving them?

A Difficult Ask

I know that for some, the idea of serving your leader is a hard concept to simply accept at face value. It may be a difficult ask of you. You may wonder, *Shouldn't my leader see me as their customer? Aren't they here to serve me?* That is a fair question.

I would say this: "Yes, they are. But they may not know that just yet. They may not have read this material or thought about things in this way."

It is amazing to me that the concept of the inverted pyramid remains foreign to most leaders. Have you ever heard about it before? A simple Google search will turn up a lot of information on it.

Maybe your leader has never been introduced to the subject. Maybe they have never studied the various leadership models we will talk about in the following pages. Maybe they are so busy trying to keep their head above water that they have never taken a moment to stop and ponder the whole idea of you being the customer. Maybe you, too, have not thought of your direct reports as your customers.

Before you go any further, let me ask you to wipe the slate clean. Let go of the angst you may have because your leader has been less than perfect. Let go of the resentment over not getting the raise or promotion you deserve. Let go of any judgement of their leadership style. Just for the time you will take to contemplate this northern vector, I would like you to suspend any and all ascribing of motive to action.

Give yourself that same grace to be a less-than-perfect leader to your people. You have not served each and every one of them to the very best of your ability. OK. Now let that go. The question to ask is, what are you going to do going forward that will make a difference in how you work together?

I know we are moving fast, and simply asking you with a few words to change any negative thinking is a very tall order. But it is possible. You can do it. A tremendous part of leadership is having the right mindset. The battle is often won or lost between your ears. Win this battle, just for today, and suspend your belief system of whose customer is whose. Just for today, see your primary customer as the leader to whom you report. Go with me on this.

What would change in your behavior if you genuinely embraced this as fact? How would your interface with your leader change? If you actually believed that your most important customer was not the one from the east, but the one from the north, what would you do differently?

With this kind of thought process, let me show you how you can best serve your primary northern stakeholder. This brings me to a concept we are all familiar with—managing up.

Managing Up

Everyone knows that you have to manage up at times to get your leader to do the things he or she needs to do. Right?

Let me confess to you that I have been teaching the principles of managing up for three-plus decades and it was not until a few years ago that I realized I had it all wrong. There is no such thing as managing up! It is a complete misnomer. Why do I say that?

Management implies control. You are a manager of people and projects. You control your direct reports' workflows, and you control your projects, at least theoretically, when they are not controlling you. In any event, as a manager, you have authority over a significant number of aspects of your people's time and your projects' functioning. Not so with your leader. You don't control anything about that person. Thinking in terms of managing up is a mistake.

"So," you might ask, "if you are not managing up, what are you doing?" Good question. The paradigm shift I had a few years ago is this: that what you are doing is actually "leading up." What is leadership if not the art of influencing others to go in a direction you believe they should go? So, you are leading your leader to do the right thing, according to what you see and believe.

Leading Up

Take this as permission to do your best to influence your leader. If you are going to act in their best interest, and that of the company, then I would say you are doing your job. If you are going to act in your own self-interest, apart from theirs, then I would say you are not. My recommendation is that you check your motives before you try to wield your influence. If they are pure, focused on the good of your leader and the good of the company, then have at it. If you are driving your own selfish agenda, wanting to make life easier for yourself, I would caution you that people can and do see through those attempts and it will hurt your relationships with those you need most to be in your corner.

Back to an earlier question: "Shouldn't my leader see me as their customer? Aren't they here to serve me?" The short answer: yes. But you need to do your part to help them. We will talk about this more later as we look at other vectors.

For now, be intentional about leading up. Do help your leader to be the best they can be. See that as part of your job. I believe they will notice what you are doing and reciprocate in kind. Magic really starts to happen when leader and direct report see each other as customers, and each tries equally hard to serve the other. This is the ideal we want to strive for.

In summary, see your direct superior as your primary customer. Work hard to make their life easier. Help them to be the best they can be by influencing up. By building this kind of quality bridge, you will ensure a free flow of communication, which will improve your customer service to this critical vector.

North-South Highway

As you reflect on your north-south relationships, you will notice that you are in the same position with your direct reports as your board, CEO or leader is with you. You are both a customer of the north, as well as a recipient of customer service from that same vector. You are a customer of your southern group of direct reports, as well as someone who has customers (direct reports) who want and need to be served.

You'll notice that everything we see applying to your leader in terms of customer service also applies to you as you serve the needs of your direct reports. This brings me to a saying worth remembering: "People join companies and leave bosses."

The degree to which your leader sees you as a customer is the degree to which you will develop loyalty to that leader. And, the degree to which you serve your direct reports and meet their needs is the degree to which they will be loyal to you. Your north-south customer highway may be analogous to an abandoned, overgrown, pothole-filled road, or conversely, a freshly asphalted, eight-lane super-highway.

The quality of the journey is heavily dependent on the quality of the relationships you have, north and south. The quality of your north-south journey is wholly dependent on you and what you make of these critical stakeholder relationships. There is no better way to have great quality relationships than to see these two vectors as customers. In the next chapter, we will specifically look at ways you can excel with your southern stakeholders to ensure your journey is as smooth as possible and that your travel is not hindered by any roadblocks, detours, or major potholes.

For Further Discussion

- When you think about the leader you report to as a customer, what thoughts come to your mind?

- If you asked this customer to rate your quality of customer service to him or her, what do you think you would hear?

- Beyond your direct leader, what other customers do you serve as you look north? What do you think they would say about the quality of your service to them?

- Have you done a good job of leading up? How can you do a better one?

- When you think about the north-south journey, how successful have you been in navigating the travel? Where are the potholes in the road? What can you do to fix them?

CHAPTER 2
SOUTH

Chapter 2: SOUTH

During the mid-eighties, the organizational development consultancy I ran was hired by Intelogic Trace to do change management. This 2,000-employee ISO (independent service organization) with IBM as its main customer was not meeting the board's expectations.

One day, I came to realize that they had much more severe problems than those I was trying to fix. The presenting problem I was asked to address was "uninspiring customer service," and the customer support division was getting hammered by John Paget, the CEO, for poor performance.

Things got so bad that Intelogic Trace was forced to do a reduction in force (RIF). John so identified with his employees that he could not pull the trigger on 1,000 employees without also putting himself in the RIF. I was amazed when he told me. Looking back, I would say that John over-identified with his southern vector and did not have great skill in keeping his northern vector informed or served. He was a classic example of "a strength overused becomes a weakness."

John called me one day telling me that he had resigned. When I asked why, he explained that he felt so bad about laying off 1,000 employees that he could not in good conscience stay. I sheepishly asked, "John, do you have a plan of where you are going or what you are going to do?"

"No," he replied.

Thus began my career coaching practice, helping the Johns of the world better plan their careers. He went on to work for Jack Welch at GE and Bob Huang at Synnex, then landed at Avnet, where our story picks up.

Example of a Servant Leader

I will never forget the first time I began coaching John at Avnet (NASDAQ: AVT), a Fortune 500 technology solutions company and distributor of electronic components. I flew into Phoenix, Arizona for our first session—this was many years after our first engagement in Intelogic Trace, but still back in the day when all my coaching was face to face and often involved a plane ride. As I walked through the lobby, I was greeted by Denise, the receptionist.

"Hi," I said. "I am Daniel Mueller, here to see John Paget."

She brightened up. "Right away, sir."

By this time in my career, I was used to the drill. I would wait a while and then be fetched to my executive's office by his or her executive assistant. But after a moment, Denise approached me. "John will be right down to get you."

"John himself is coming down to get me?" I hardly believed my ears. In the hallowed grounds of the executive suite of the Fortune 500, this was simply not done.

I was feeling very special until Denise burst my bubble: "John always comes down to get all his guests."

"All his guests?" I stammered. *How is that possible? He is a super-busy executive in his first three months as executive vice president of a major company.* Denise seemed to be beaming, so my instinct kicked in and I asked, "Tell me, how do you like John?"

"Oh, he is wonderful. He is so wonderful."

"Why is that?" I probed.

"Well, he is always asking me how I am doing. And you know, I can tell he really cares. And he takes time to know about me. He even remembers my children's names, and always asks about them."

"Wow, that is amazing," I agreed.

Just then, John showed up. As I followed him down a long corridor and up to the second floor—it took a good five-minute walk to reach the office on Executive Row—I asked, "You have some hike to get downstairs and back. How do you find the time? Why don't you send your assistant?"

John made very direct, intense eye contact with me, and said, "Mary has a lot of work to do. I don't want to disturb her."

Authenticity Is a Must

Interesting, I thought. This guy really does believe in serving others. Even the little people. It's as if he is treating them like I was just treated. Like a customer.

It was then that something unusual on his bookshelf caught my attention. "John, what is this?" I asked. While most executives have their favorite books on their bookcase, John had gone a few steps further. He had at least a dozen copies of the same book. "Do you recommend this book?" I stupidly asked.

Only now, as I am writing about this event several decades later, do I realize how silly of a question that was. Of course he recommends the book! He has twelve copies of it, you idiot!

John was gracious. "Yes. I think it is one of the best business books ever written, and I give it out to all my direct reports." Well, John was a rock star in my world, and if he recommended it, that was good enough for me.

In the jacket of *Stewardship: Choosing Service Over Self-Interest*, John wrote a nice note to me which was the spark that began a lifelong relationship with this amazing executive who worked for the Jack Welches (GE) and John Sculleys (Apple) of the world. Wherever John went for the next two decades, my coaching firm and I would soon follow, until he retired and came to work for me as a coach. Everywhere John went, frontline employees had good things to say about him. He was the champion of the frontline employee. He saw that person as truly important and significant.

In *Stewardship*, first published in 1993, Block talks about what it takes to be a good steward of what we have been entrusted with.

> *Stewardship is a way to use power to serve through the practice of partnership and empowerment. This is the alternative to the conventional notions of "strong leadership" for implementing changes. The intent is to redesign our organizations so that service is the centerpiece and ownership, and responsibility are strongly felt among those close to doing the work and contacting customers.[3]*

Before you click to download on Amazon, I am not telling you that this is the best book I have ever read. It is not. What I am saying is that this inspired a very powerful, top-down, command-and-control executive to be deeply committed to redefining who a customer is, and to become passionate about serving those who reported to him—as passionate as he was with his external customers, on whom he depended equally to keep the lights on.

John passed away several years ago. At his funeral, person after person got up to talk about the incredible impact he made in people's lives. He truly had a servant's heart and did in fact embody the subtitle of Block's book: *Choosing Service Over Self-Interest.*

That said, he did have a blind spot that I could never help him uncover. His relationships to the north were never that great. John was a champion of his people, and they loved him for it. However, he was let go quite often as a result of failed relationships with

---

3 Peter Block, Stewardship: Choosing Service Over Self-Interest (San Francisco: Berrett-Koehler Publishers, Inc., 1993), 63.

his bosses, whom he saw as not caring enough about his primary customer, his direct reports. He over-indexed on his southern vector.

What if They Don't Get It?

Some instantly get this compass metaphor, and it changes their paradigm. They see where they are over-indexing and stop it. They are what I call "quick studies." Some are set in their ways, like John, and do a great job in three of the four vectors, but miss achieving their full potential because of a blind spot in one area.

For example, not everyone will get or embrace the concept of treating direct reports as customers. I will never forget the conversation several years ago when Mary (not her real name), head of HR, was receiving coach-the-coach by me, helping her coach one of the senior executives on her team. She administered our executive competencies assessment and was doing a debrief. There are five categories of executive competency identified: Core Character, Execution, Relationship, Management, and Leadership. Mary relayed to me as she was debriefing this person that she noticed their lowest score was in the Core Character section. This executive had given themselves a zero on servant leadership.

Mary probed, asking, "What can you do to improve this score?"

The executive immediately exclaimed, "Being a servant leader does not sound good at all to me! Why would I want to become that?"

Wow, I thought. *I guess this concept is not well received by everyone!*

So, what were the concepts that caused this executive to have such a visceral reaction? We can look to what Wikipedia says for clues:

Servant leadership is a leadership philosophy in which the main goal of the leader is to serve. This is different from traditional leadership where the leader's main focus is the thriving of their company or organizations. A servant leader shares power, puts the needs of the employees first and helps people develop and perform as highly as possible. Servant leadership inverts the norm, which puts the customer service associates as a main priority. Instead of the people working to serve the leader, the leader exists to serve the people.[4]

Who Likely Rejects This Model?

Executives who have worked their entire careers to achieve a position of power and control are turned off to the concept of servant leadership. So was the case with Mary's executive. The good news is that as a result of our work, Mary realized she was going to be limited in her ability to effectively coach this executive and brought us in to provide a coach. Hopefully, this will help. At the time of writing, the jury is still out, but we are encouraged because the CEO is now involved and sponsoring the engagement, so there is top-down visibility into the process and an expectation that this executive will improve their approach to leadership. Time will tell.

Servant Leadership Defined

So, this begs the question: "What exactly is servant leadership?" In preparation for writing this rapid-read book, I did two types of research for this chapter. First, I Googled "direct report as customer." Then, "employee as customer." Finding nothing of value, I tried many other permutations, without luck. So, I gave up, and Googled "servant leader" knowing I would find a treasure trove of great thinking on the subject. I've concluded there is a

4 "Servant leadership," Wikipedia, Wikimedia Foundation, Inc., last modified January 23, 2021, https://en.wikipedia.org/wiki/Servant_leadership.

strong need for more publishing on the subject of your direct reports being seen as your customers. However, the concept of servant leadership is very much in line with this paradigm, so for a moment let's explore this leadership model in greater depth.

First of all, servant leadership is only one model of leadership. It is NOT the best model, nor is it the ONLY model. Models are useful when discussing leadership, because you can neatly define what leadership is and what it is not. However, models are less useful in the field as you, the leader, are executing on a day-to-day basis. I strongly believe a **blended** approach to leadership, using a number of different models, is the very best approach. For those with a top-down leadership style, studying and embracing servant leadership will help you improve dramatically in your southern relationships.

Example of a Servant Leader

Servant leaders are the antithesis of top-down leaders. Bharath Oruganti, SVP of Service Delivery at Q2 Software, is a great example of a servant leader. Because he is a servant leader, who naturally wants to focus on others instead of himself, I am sure he is squirming as he reads this. I can already hear the conversation I will have with him as he reviews my book.

> *Daniel, I like all that you wrote except the part where you talk about me. Take that out. I don't want this to be about me. Focus on others. Can't you use some other person as an example? I am really not all that you are making me out to be.*

My answer:

> *No. You are a real-time example of an effective leader who uses this blended approach for maximum effectiveness. I really need to tell your story. Sorry.*

Bharath takes the traditional power leadership model and flips it upside down. He tries to put the people actually doing the delivery work at the top of the hierarchy and puts himself and his leaders at the bottom. He is unconscious of this. It is just his style. This has not been an intellectual choice of his, based on studying a number of leadership models and then choosing to be a servant leader. No, I would suggest to you that he came out of the womb with that predisposition, over time was nurtured in this vein, and has received a lot of positive reinforcement along the way as a result of significant career success.

Now, I am not saying he is a perfect leader. By no means. Every leader has areas in which to grow. I am simply pointing out that he has a "serve-first" mindset, where he is focused on empowering and uplifting those who work for him. He tends to serve others instead of taking a command-and-control approach. He demonstrates a certain degree of humility instead of wielding authority, and frequently looks for ways to develop his staff and unlock their potential, creativity, and sense of purpose. For example, Bharath gave me three of his employees to coach in 2020.

As I reported back progress on the coaching of Kyle, Bill, and Mitchell, Bharath's questions were always around each person's development for their highest and best good first, and then secondarily, the good of Q2 Software.

"What is the result of such an approach?" you may wonder.

"Performance goes through the roof," says Art Barter, founder and CEO of the Servant Leadership Institute and CEO of Datron World Communications, Inc.

"Magic happens," agrees Patricia Falotico, a former executive leader at IBM who is now CEO of the Robert K. Greenleaf Center for Servant Leadership (*https://www.greenleaf.org/*).

What Is the Big Difference?

"What is the difference between most business leaders and a servant leader?" you may ask. A traditional business leader often sees themselves in a transactional relationship.

To quote one, "I see myself in a taskmaster role, where I have to achieve desired performance levels from my people, and as a result my people receive compensation. I am the boss, and they are my vehicle for executing results and hitting my objectives." This "positional leadership" mindset leaves out the idea of servant leadership, which moves the leader beyond transactional management.

A servant leader:

1. Has a strong desire to align each direct report's sense of purpose with the organization's mission.

2. Empathetically and actively listens to the needs of stakeholders with genuine care and concern.

3. Sees their role as one of stewardship, taking care of entrusted resources.

4. Leads by example, role-modeling behavior and persuading others to emulate.

5. Focuses on others and not on the self with a fair degree of altruism and other-centeredness.

The results of this approach include:

- A humble leader who is adept at influencing followers through positive character traits.

- Empowered staff performing at a higher, more innovative level.

- Employees feeling more engaged and purpose-driven, which in turn increases the organization's retention and lowers turnover.

- Well-trained and trusted direct reports continuing to develop as future leaders, thus helping to ensure the long-term viability of the organization.

I'm in! Where Do I Start?

Assuming you have been persuaded to add a servant leadership mindset to your leadership style, where do you start and what actions should you take?

Firstly, you need to make sure you are not about to give yourself permission to over-index on serving your southern vector to the detriment of other vectors. Those who get most excited about this model are those who are already servant leaders. Be careful. You need to be equally strong in all four vectors.

Secondly, if this is a growth opportunity for you, let go of any selfish motivations you may have. Your focus on meeting your own needs has to decrease, and your focus on meeting those of your stakeholders needs to increase.

Thirdly, realize that you need to serve all four vectors. One of my criticisms of the servant leadership model is that it is too focused on serving in the southerly direction.

The truth is that the best leaders serve omnidirectionally. This is not to say that they are doormats, allowing others to walk on them or take advantage of this other-centered approach to leading. Sometimes, the best way to serve someone is to call them out, remind them in no uncertain terms of a boundary you have set, or let them go. Being a servant leader does not mean being a pushover.

Example of a Servant Leadership Company

Southwest Airlines, under the guidance of CEO Gary Kelly, is frequently cited as the model servant leadership corporation. Southwest's culture of putting employees first has resulted in a highly engaged, low-turnover workforce, and in 2020 it reported its forty-seventh consecutive year of profitability! It is a real-world practical example of what can be achieved with this leadership approach.

Kelly is a product of the Southwest culture. He first joined Southwest Airlines in 1986 as a controller. In 1989, Kelly was promoted to CFO and VP Finance. In 2001, he was named EVP, and then promoted to his current position as CEO and Vice Chairman in 2004.

This "promotion from within" success story is eclipsed by Southwest's President Emeritus, Colleen C. Barrett. Co-founder Herb Kelleher's story is equally inspiring. Both these stories are worth looking into for any aspirational leader. A simple Wikipedia search will suffice.

In 1996, Kevin and Jackie Freiberg wrote a national bestseller, *Nuts! Southwest Airlines' Crazy Recipe for Business and Personal Success.*

In it they write:

> *It has become rather fashionable in management circles to talk about the concept of service or servant leadership. Robert Greenleaf's magnificent book Servant Leadership has become a landmark in the management and leadership literature. It makes sense. After all, the idea has been tested for a couple of millennia. The concept suggests that inherent in the act of leadership is the natural desire and corresponding choice to first serve others. The defining element lies in a person's first inclination: is it to lead*

or is it to serve? The first inclination of great leaders is servanthood. Most people are drawn to leadership because they feel compelled to serve a purpose larger than themselves.

What seems to be missing from the mainstream discussions about servant leadership is the tremendous sacrifice that often comes with choosing to be a servant first. The people of Southwest Airlines have not achieved great success without paying a significant price. What goes on behind the scenes is a tremendous amount of hard work and self-sacrifice. Barrett and Kelleher routinely put in sixteen-hour days and regularly work seven days a week. While they don't require that level of commitment from others, the travel schedules and workloads are grueling for most people at Southwest. For some the sacrifice is offset by how much fun they have at work. However, we would be remiss in not telling you that, for some Southwest employees, something is forfeited.5

When leaders think about putting their people first and serving them, especially macho leaders who are heavily focused on command and control, they can sometimes see this as a weak form of leadership.

However, as stated earlier, this is definitely not the case. Kevin and Jackie Freiberg go on to write:

Servanthood is anything but weak. We seriously doubt that former Braniff CEO Harding Lawrence or former Texas International CEO Frank Lorenzo view Herb Kelleher as soft or weak. Yet, ask people inside or outside the company and they will tell you that Herb's first inclination is to subordinate his own interests to those of Southwest

---

5 Kevin L. Freiberg and Jacquelyn A. Freiberg, *Nuts! Southwest Airlines' Crazy Recipe for Business and Personal Success* (New York: Bard Books, 1996), 310.

Airlines. This is certainly consistent with Kelleher's own philosophy: "Leadership is being a faithful, devoted, hard-working servant of the people you lead and participating with them in the agonies as well as the ecstasies of life."[6]

If you are interested in additional reading on the subject, start with a simple Google search and you will find tons of information. You will notice Robert Greenleaf's 1971 essay, *"The Servant as Leader,"* mentioned a lot. In addition, you will see quite a bit about the Atlanta-based Greenleaf Center for Servant Leadership. However, Greenleaf is by no means the creator of this model, as the very earliest leaders in the history of mankind espoused these values in no uncertain terms.

Since becoming popular in the seventies and eighties, there has been extensive research on the subject and many case studies, like that of Southwest Airlines, that have proven conclusively that this is a highly effective leadership model. That said, to my earlier point, a blended approach seems to work best overall. I would suggest studying other leadership frameworks as well. While I don't have time to get into the various other models here, suffice it to say that there is more to it than having a framework. You also need, for example, to understand the behavioral sciences and how to navigate them in order to be effective at using your customer compass.

The Behavioral Sciences

For a moment, I would like to dive into the behavioral sciences and how they relate to you serving your customers.

As you likely know, each person tends to have behavioral preferences—preferred ways of behaving.

Through simple observation, and through assessments, you can

---

6 Freiberg and Freiberg, *Nuts*, 311.

identify these behavioral preferences. For this book's purposes, I will use the D-I-S-C model that I developed in the mid-eighties, as I studied many other DISC-related models.

Each expert in the field calls the quadrants by different names but is describing the same common sets of behaviors.

SOLID's DISC Model

My model, like others, identifies the four major quadrants of behavior, with identification of a primary and secondary preferred style.

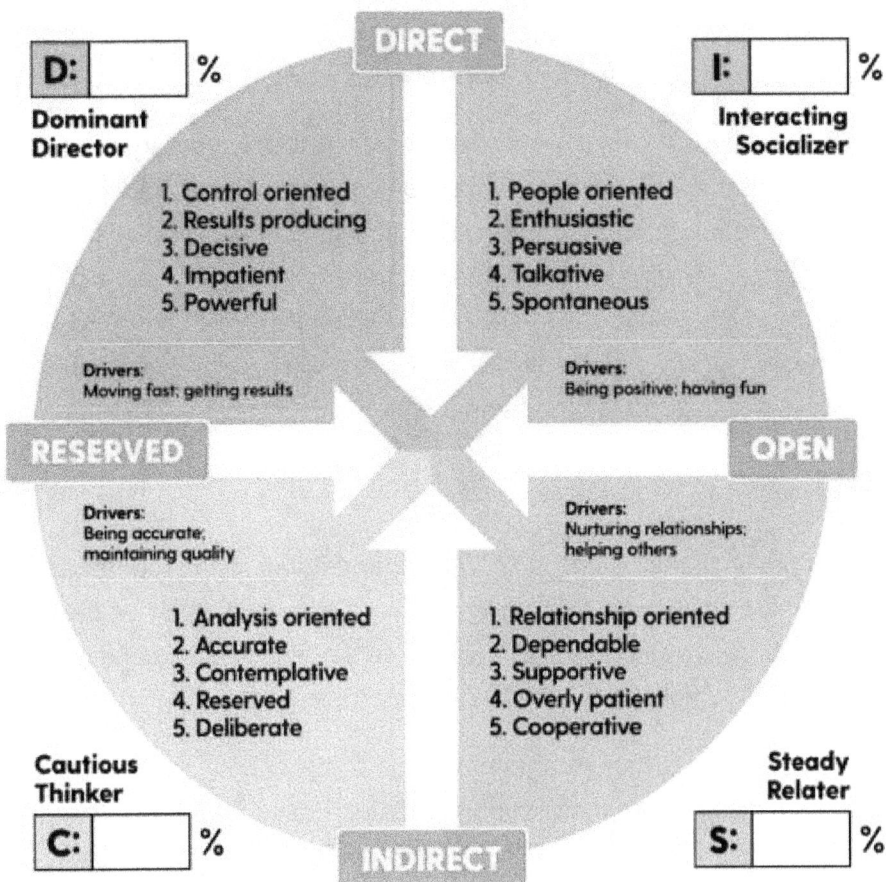

D: [   ] %

Dominant Director

DIRECT

I: [   ] %

Interacting Socializer

1. Control oriented
2. Results producing
3. Decisive
4. Impatient
5. Powerful

1. People oriented
2. Enthusiastic
3. Persuasive
4. Talkative
5. Spontaneous

Drivers:
Moving fast; getting results

Drivers:
Being positive; having fun

RESERVED

OPEN

Drivers:
Being accurate;
maintaining quality

Drivers:
Nurturing relationships;
helping others

1. Analysis oriented
2. Accurate
3. Contemplative
4. Reserved
5. Deliberate

1. Relationship oriented
2. Dependable
3. Supportive
4. Overly patient
5. Cooperative

Cautious Thinker

Steady Relater

C: [   ] %

INDIRECT

S: [   ] %

D stands for **Dominant Director**. Those with this primary style tend to prefer a direct, decisive, results-oriented approach to leadership.

I stands for **Interacting Socializer**, and those with this primary style tend to prefer an engaging, upbeat, positive and enthusiastic style of leadership. Those with a strong D preference and a secondary I, or vice versa, tend to prefer an inspirational style of leadership, combining their two preferences.

S stands for **Steady Relater**, and those with this primary preference tend to take a steady, relational, empathetic, and highly nurturing approach to leadership. Those with a strong I preference, and a secondary S, or vice versa, tend to be highly people- and relationship-centric in their leadership and put a major emphasis on team cohesiveness, comradery, and harmony.

C stands for **Cautious Thinker**, and those with this primary style tend to prefer a very deliberate, methodical, and carefully planned approach to leadership. Those with a strong S preference with a secondary C, or vice versa, tend to have a more subtle, indirect, tactful, and diplomatic leadership style, while those with a high C, secondary D, or vice versa, tend to have a more reserved, results-oriented and task-driven leadership style.

Is There a Best Style for Leadership?

Behaviorally speaking, there is no best leadership style. You have your preferred way of interacting with people, and each of the combinations we just discussed can be very effective at influencing people in the direction in which you want them to go.

That said, there are several things to note when it comes to your leadership style in the light of your behavior. Firstly, that it is critical that you have an accurate understanding of your own behavioral preferences. Secondly, we all tend to see reality through the filter of our own behavioral style. We often project our style onto others, and consciously or unconsciously prefer people who exhibit behaviors similar to those we prefer. Thirdly, that it is the leader's job to adapt their style to meet the needs of others, and not the other way around. I call this trait "adaptability" and believe that the best leaders are those who are the most capable and willing to adapt their style to meet the needs of their customers, north, south, east, and west.

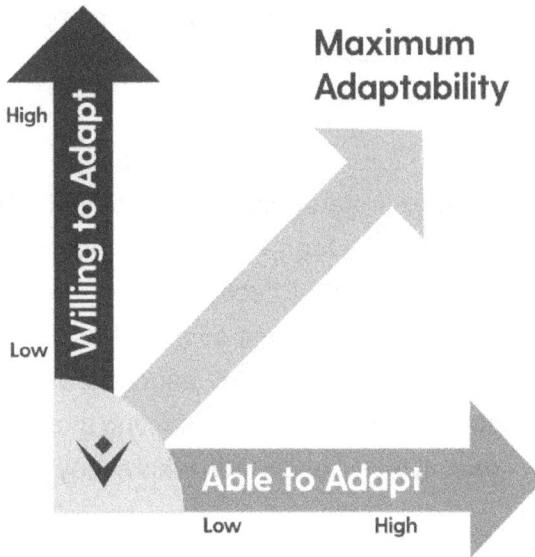

Practical Application

As a leader, a practical application of the behavioral sciences in relationship to your leadership style includes the following two key points:

1. You need to ensure that you are WILLING to adapt your style to meet others' needs. This involves a paradigm shift from "My direct reports are here to meet my goals and objectives" to one of "I exist to serve my people and help them to achieve their goals and objectives. As such, I am willing to adapt my behavioral style to better meet their needs." This takes humility and a servant leadership stance more than it takes training. It is a mindset.

2. You need to ensure you are ABLE to adapt your style to meet others' needs. In order to do this, you need to understand your own behavioral preferences, identify the behavioral style of the person you are attempting to influence and lead, and be able adapt your style to their behavioral preference when communicating with them. This takes intentionality, conscious thought, and a sensitivity to other styles. But above all, it takes training. Otherwise, you will be unaware of your strong propensity for your own style and miss the opportunity to adapt to better meet the needs of others.

In order to reach full effectiveness, leaders need maximum adaptability. An inaccurate understanding of their own behavioral tendencies will weaken a leader's ability to effectively adapt their style to the needs of others. Effective leaders are able to develop or improve positive relationships in much less time than would normally be needed. Most effective leaders are unconsciously or consciously adept at identifying and adapting their leadership style to the behavioral style of people with whom they work.

That said, it is unfortunate that most learning in the behavioral sciences stops there. I call it navel gazing. I blame consultants and coaches for leading you astray in this area. You gain great insight into your own style, and to the styles of your teammates. But little attention, if any, is given to helping you practice adapting your style to meet others' needs. I believe this final part is the most important.

Knowing yourself is useful only if it is going to result in making you a more adaptable leader, better understanding what makes people tick, north, south, east, and west.

Without that focus, you will keep your customer compass in your pocket, and be at a disadvantage as you seek to omnidirectionally serve your stakeholders.

As I think about this last sentence, the thought crossed my mind: *If I were to re-title this book, I would call it Stakeholder-Centered Customer Service.*

What do you think?

Serving Your People

As you look south, you now see your direct reports, to a greater or lesser degree, in a different light.

The next logical question is, "What now?

What do I do to better serve my people?" Great question.

Michael Timmes, a human resources consultant with Insperity, Inc. (NASDAQ: NSP), is an often-quoted expert on applied servant leadership.

As you, the leader, develop customers in your southern vector—your direct reports—you would hear him say:

> *It is critical to maintain a continual focus on developing your people. You need to be spending at least 20% of your time in people development. If you are not doing that, you are not doing your job.*

He recently posted this picture of Helen, which pretty much sums up the approach that great leaders strive to take as they interface with those they lead.

For me, I would say it goes beyond kindness and looks more like tough love. Here is how a kickoff, developmental one-on-one meeting may go:

_____(Name), I like you and I want you to be successful, so I am going to start being much more intentional about developing you into the leader you need to be. Therefore, we are going to start with an honest and candid appraisal of your strengths and weaknesses. I am going to call them out as I see them, and this may be a little painful at times, but in order for me to effectively serve you and help you grow, I need to be totally straight with you._

Some of what you see as your strengths are actually being overused and are turning into weaknesses. Some of what you perceive as your strengths are not really your strengths at all, and some of the things you do that you don't realize are your strengths, are in fact some of your greatest assets.

On the weaknesses side, you have some blind spots. I know. You don't see them. That is why they are called blind spots. And some of your weaknesses you are actually minimizing and are creating elaborate excuses to avoid looking at them. You need to face them head-on and grow.

To that end, I am going to be meeting with you once per month for a pure developmental one-on-one, where I am going to be very intentional about developing you. Now, I am going to invest my time into serving you like this, and it is going to be a sacrifice, because this one hour a month is precious, so I need you to treat it as such.

Finally, there are three rules in the developmental work we are going to do together.

Rule 1: You are responsible for doing all the work in these developmental meetings. Rule 2: All the responsibility for the prep work for these meetings is on you. Rule 3: If and when you are wondering what to do, see rules 1 and 2. Smile.

This speech may sound overly direct to some. But I guarantee you, your A-players are going to sit straight up, see the tremendous gift for what it is, smile, and get to work, taking advantage of your kind willingness to invest yourself in their development.

Your B-players are going to be interested in hearing you talk about their strengths, wish you would not bring up their weaknesses, and come into each session half as prepared as your A-players.

Your C-players are going to come in unprepared for their monthly developmental one-on-one, fail to see the value, and wonder if you are going to take some things off their plate so they have time to prepare for these burdensome meetings.

Your direct report's reaction to you doing developmental one-on-ones is a reliable indicator of the level at which they play IF you are being an effective leader and manager for them. If you are a jerk or a poor performance manager, then all bets are off.

Your job in these developmental one-one-ones is to ask the right questions. Not enough can be said on the merits of using the Socratic method of asking provocative questions, listening carefully between the lines of what is being said, and accurately reflecting back what you are hearing and seeing. Great question-asking and excellent listening skills are hallmarks of a great leader, and they serve to build deeper, higher-trust relationships with direct reports than lectures, demands, and treating the person as a human doing rather than a human being.

Delegation

Another major area of practical application is in delegation. How and what you delegate to your people really matters. It is one of the most common developmental areas executives work on no matter what their level: director, senior director, VP, SVP, C-suite, or CEO. It makes sense. As you go to the next level of functional effectiveness, you have to let go of things that you were previously doing so you have capacity to take on new responsibilities. In order to take on more, you have to delegate more of your responsibilities to others, normally your direct reports.

The process of delegation is a very powerful tool for driving effective customer service to all your vectors. It is not just about getting the work off your plate and onto someone else's. It is a way for you to selectively give up power and control so that your direct reports can take the lead in various projects and functions, thereby taking greater ownership of organizational initiatives. Delegation is a very strong talent development tool and a proven process for succession. It also grows you as a leader in many ways.

For more than three decades, I have been providing delegation coaching as a core part of my executive development practice, and it never gets old. It is very exciting to see a leader let go of certain responsibilities, empowering others to take the reins, while my leader takes on new, expanded, and usually more strategic responsibilities. Make it your aim to grow your direct reports in such a way that more of your day-to-day responsibilities are done by them. This will progressively free you up to work at higher and higher levels.

A Key to Promotion

One of the number-one reasons I see people getting promoted is because they are good at delegation and have effectively empowered their team, freeing their leader up for added responsibility. Conversely, one of the number-one reasons I see for promotion remaining elusive is the inability to let go of tactical details that are better done by direct reports.

As I start to coach someone, I have a conversation with their boss. Hundreds of times I have heard things like "she is too in the weeds … too hands on" or "he is too tactical and not strategic enough."

Well, to solve that issue, appropriate delegation is needed. And "appropriate" is the operative word here. Delegation is not a process of dumping things you don't want to do or don't have time for on your staff. There is definitely an art and a science to this process.

We won't go into the details of the "how" here, but suffice it to say that delegation should be something every leader studies and consciously works on to improve their effectiveness. It just so happens that this is an ideal tool as you are trying to improve your customer service to your southern vector.

Accountability

Although I really want to wrap up this section and ensure this rapid-read book remains rapid-read, I feel compelled to talk about accountability because it is an integral and critical part of effective delegation.

Accountability is to delegation as your quadricep (front of your upper leg) is to your hamstring (back of your upper leg). These two muscles are known as an opposing muscle group. If you were any type of professional athlete, and you had a good sports and fitness coach, you would be working them both out in a balanced way. Why? Because if you overwork one muscle group, say, your quads, and ignore your hamstring, it will actually weaken the entire structure. You will be unbalanced and highly predisposed to pull your hamstring, which is most painful and debilitating. So, too, if you are not strong in accountability, then your delegation muscle will be weak. In fact, the number-one reason I see leaders struggle with delegation is because they have a weak or absent accountability system.

So, in summary, being strong in holding your people accountable for what they say they are going to do is the mark of a top leader. Without that skill, my experience is that you will be reticent to delegate for fear that what you delegate will not get done in the time in which you need it. There are many more factors to consider in both these disciplines, of course, but these are two critical skills to master as you serve your customer to the south.

For Additional Learning

You likely have many questions. Good. Explore online and company resources for more information and learning in these areas. But let's address some of the concerns you may have about fully embracing the idea of serving your direct reports. For example, what about control? Namely, would you not lose control if you gave up too much, were very empowering, and gave more and more responsibility away? Actually, no, you would not. The inverse is true. You would have more control in a deeper sense, because your people would control their areas of responsibility with greater ownership and commitment, which would free up your time to focus on those things that only you can address.

Another concern you may have is being replaced. You might wonder, *If I do such a great job designing accountability systems and delegating work that I am not needed, will management get rid of me?*

The answer is "No" to this also. You will instead become more valuable and more strategic, and thereby more promotable and more likely to receive bonuses, raises, and promotions.

Putting It All Together

Let me pull this all together with a true success story. Back in 2001, I provided coaching to Dan Rourke, a junior at Cadence Design Systems (NASDAQ: CDNS). He worked for the VP of Services, Pat McCarty. Dan and Pat developed a very high-trust relationship. She wanted to go to the next level and realized that developing Dan would be instrumental in paving the way for her promotion, as well as his. So, she mentored Dan and had regular developmental one-on-ones with him. She also hired me to coach him. Together, we tag-teamed on Dan's development.

Meanwhile, Dan worked hard on growing his people. He put simple but effective accountability systems in place that tracked tasks and actions, he delegated an ever-increasing amount of responsibility to his managers, and he occasionally brought people like me in to work with his team.

Eventually, Pat was promoted to SVP, Dan was promoted to VP, and we started working on developing his next-in-line, Neil Kenagy, much the same way as Pat did with Dan. When Dan left Cadence, Neil was eventually promoted to Group Director of Service Delivery, where he was also intentional about developing his direct reports.For the full case study, see the Appendix.

Critical Ingredients for a Successful North-South Corridor

What were the critical ingredients in the relationship with Dan and Pat? Here is what I saw:

1. High trust between leader and direct report.

2. The willingness on the part of the mentee to be open, coachable, and teachable.

3. The selflessness on the part of the leader to build into the direct report over time.

4. A good degree of patience on everyone's part, because this process took years, not months.

5. Humility. Sue, Dan and Neil would all be described as humble.

6. Encouragement of the growth of the next level while making a point of being intentional about the process.

7. A genuine desire for what was best for their direct report, and the reciprocation of that intention.

Of these seven important ingredients, number one is "high trust." It is the kind of trust described by Patrick Lencioni in the national bestseller *The Advantage*. Patrick talks about the critical need for trust as he makes his case that the marketplace "advantage" any organization can attain is that of organizational health.

> *The kind of trust that is necessary to build a great team is what I call vulnerability-based trust. This is what happens when members get to a point where they are completely comfortable being transparent, honest, and naked with one another, where they say and genuinely mean things like "I screwed up," "I need help," "Your idea is better than mine," "I wish I could learn to do that as well as you do," and even "I'm sorry." ... At the heart of vulnerability lies the willingness of people to abandon their pride and their fear, to sacrifice their egos for the collective good of the team.[7]*

Can you be transparent and vulnerable with your customers to the north? Can you abandon your pride and be open with your customers to the south? What is the quality of your north-south corridor?

As you reflect on your relationships to your north, on a scale of 1–10, with 10 = Total Trust, rate your relationship with your leader. Now reflect on your southern relationships.

Think through each one of your direct reports. Using that same scale, how would they rate you?

---

7 Patrick Lencioni, *The Advantage: Why Organizational Health Trumps Everything Else in Business* (San Francisco: Jossey-Bass, 2012), 27.

Trust Changes Everything

In Stephen M.R. Covey's *The Speed of Trust: The One Thing that Changes Everything*, he writes:

> *The truth is that in every relationship—personal and professional—what you do has far greater impact than anything you say. You can say you love someone—but unless you demonstrate that love through your actions, your words become meaningless. You can say you want to engage in win-win negotiation—but unless your behavior shows that you really mean it, you will come across as insincere. You can say your company puts the customer first. You can say that you recognize people as your most important asset. You can say that you will comply with the rules, that you won't engage in unethical practices, that you will respect a confidence, keep a commitment, or deliver results. You can say all of these things, but unless you actually do them, your words will not build trust; in fact, they will destroy it. Good words have their place. They signal behavior. They declare intent. They can create enormous hope. And when those words are followed by validating behavior, they increase trust, sometimes dramatically. But when the behavior doesn't follow or doesn't match the verbal message, words turn into withdrawals.[8]*

The point: Be careful what you say to your leader and your direct reports. As you navigate north-south, recognize that your words are not important unless they are followed up consistently by action that your words indicated. If you struggle with matching your actions to your words, it is better you remain quiet and keep your work on these principles to yourself until you have improved.

---

8 Stephen M. R. Covey, *The Speed of Trust: The One Thing That Changes Everything* (New York: Free Press, 2006), 132-133.

According to Covey, trust is both a defining characteristic and defining outcome of servant leadership. It is one of the means to achieve servant leadership, and it is also an end that is achieved by servant leadership. Not every north-south relationship you have will work as well as Pat, Dan and Neil's did. However, this should be an aspirational goal of yours, to leave a legacy of those whom you have grown to the next level of functional effectiveness.

I am convinced that when you look back on your career, you will see the people you have grown as the most significant achievements of your journey. Those you have grown and developed will see you in the same way. Taking these as your bearings will assure you of the richest, most fulfilling, and most rewarding adventure as you travel the road to the next level of leadership effectiveness.

For Further Discussion

- As you reflect on your southern vector, can you see your direct reports as customers?

- If you treated your employees as customers, would they be better or worse off?

- What do you think would happen?

- What is the quality of your north-south corridor? How can you make the navigation back and forth smoother for all concerned?

CHAPTER 3

EAST

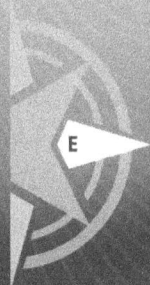

Chapter 3: EAST

It was too early for a customer call. I had been up the night before celebrating the release of my first book: *Training Skills for LEADERS.*

You could say I celebrated a little too much if you wanted to be polite. But in 1990 that is not how I would have described my inebriated condition of the night before. Colorful description aside, I was in no mood to talk to Shauna, a low-level HR employee at Dell Computers.

I had been commissioned by Dell to develop the core curriculum for Dell University, and this 187-page fully illustrated book was my ticket to the C-suite where all of the high-paying executive coaching was taking place.

Larger than life and full of myself, you could say that I was the antithesis of a servant leader at that time. I wanted to be with the important people, like Michael and his crew. Dropping his name as a coaching client would surely get me into the C-suite of other major companies.

I was fast-tracking myself to a major disaster but had no idea the light at the end of my success tunnel was a train—until it was too late.

Hitting the Wall

I was teaching classes on the subject of incidental learning to Dell's leadership, using the **L-E-A-D-E-R-S** framework I created for leaders to develop other leaders in the workplace.

Listen. Evaluate. Adopt. Deliver. Esteem. Reinforce. Serve. These seven steps to developing leaders were transformational for Dell.

It was too bad they were only head knowledge for me. If I had been able to practice these principles, my phone call that morning would have had a very different outcome. But alas, I was nowhere close to being a good leader. I was a top-down autocratic wannabe leader who thought the way to get results was through power and control.

Shauna was an impediment to my plans. She wanted to control the classes I was teaching and put guardrails in place. She did not understand my brilliance. She did not appreciate my relationships at the highest levels of Dell. She didn't understand I was too important to have to answer to her.

Ouch. This truth is painful to write. What happened next is even more cringeworthy.

"Hi Shauna. This is Daniel. What do you need?"

"Hi Daniel. How are you doing?"

"OK. What can I do for you?"

"Well, I wanted to go over our guidelines for implementing your program at Dell University. For security purposes, I need you to sign some releases, and you need to send me a copy of your contract."

"Shauna, can't you just work through my admin? We have to get these courses started and I don't have time for dealing with these details."

"Daniel, I know you think you don't have time to deal with me, but I have an important job to do."

"Shauna, that is what I pay my admin for. Can't she deal with this?"

"Well, I am sorry you don't want to deal with me. I will relay that to my boss."

"Great. I will have my admin call you to get this program moving."

As soon as we hung up, Shauna called her boss. Apparently, I was mistaken, and this person was considered a rock star inside of Dell and reported directly to the head of HR. Double ouch.

From what I understood next, Shauna communicated in no uncertain terms that she would not deal with me anymore because I disrespected her. In her view, I came across as an arrogant, egotistical prima donna. She was correct! A few days later I got a call from her boss, informing me that they would take the program I designed and implement it themselves, without my help, and that I was not needed anymore.

I had just been fired from a six-figures-a-year account, and in 1990 dollars, that was a lot of money. Do you think I learned my lesson? Nope. I had the "ism" of alcoholism. Many leaders I work with have that "ism" too. At the core of the "ism" is often selfish, self-centered behavior. For me, I had two ways of maladaptive coping: alcohol and work. If you have the "ism," it may take the form of "workaholism." But the symptoms are similar. There is some type of pain, and the medication for that pain is food, work, alcohol, control, or who knows what. It is less important how I came to that point in time. It is more important what I would choose to do about it. Sadly, I chose to do nothing.

Shrugging off the loss, I moved on. Several data points and six years later, it became obvious I had a problem, and March 4, 1996 is my sobriety date. Since then, I have completely abstained from alcohol. I also have not overworked. Well, uh, OK… I slip from time to time on overworking, like right now when I am trying to write this book in a few weeks. My butt hurts!

Back to my story. On that day in 1996, I began an inner journey to discover my purpose, mission, values, and more. As a result, I discovered the truths I am sharing here that have helped me to change. I can honestly say I have worked daily toward that end for the past several decades. And I must be a very slow learner, because I still have a long way to go to reach the place where I will be most effective as a leader. But it is progress, not perfection. Seeing customers in every vector does not come easily to people like me. My weakest area is my southern one, and my staff would tell you I am good at apologizing. Unfortunately, I get a lot of practice.

Whoever you are, you have one vector where you are super-strong. You are likely strong in a couple other vectors as well. But you also likely have an area that is weaker than the others and needs to be addressed.

Slow Progress Demands Patience

The progress has been slow. Core character defects die hard. Mine was simple: I wanted to be served. Even when I was looking east, I still saw the customer as someone who should serve me. Shauna was "low-level" in my book. She was there to meet my needs. I did not see her as a partner. I have made the same mistake with my direct reports.

The whole notion of "low-level" is wrong. Without the frontline individual contributors and managers to the south, east, and west, we could not do our jobs. They are not the "little people," nor are they "insignificant" by any stretch. They matter greatly and I need to care as much about them as I do about the stakeholders to the north.

What about you? Are you a champion of the people on the front lines? Do you treat them with the same respect as those in higher-level positions of responsibility? Do you find yourself treating your customers in the C-suite better than you do those on the front line? If so, would you like to change that?

Today, more than ever, I want to see all people as those I am here to serve. Intellectually, I know it is not just the C-suite customers who are important. Equally important are those people in the bowels of our customers who have very important jobs to do. They are trying the best they can to do what they are asked to do. We want them to be treated as well as the CEO or senior executive who is sponsoring the customer engagement. Is this a lofty goal? Yes! Is it worth striving for? You bet.

Becoming Level-Blind

How often are we more concerned with meeting our goals and objectives, and less concerned with effectively partnering with our external customers to ensure everyone's work flows more smoothly, efficiently, and pleasantly? Today more than ever, I try to be kind and supportive to those I used to see as "low-level" and less significant. Back then, these people were there to make sure my engagements went smoothly. Today, I see these operations people as partners without whom I could not succeed in delivering revenue.

Does what I am describing strike a familiar chord inside you? Do you or someone you know see the customer from two vantage points: those who are important to make happy and those who are not? Does this bifurcation work? I think not. And if it is working for you now, I believe that will be short-lived. In short, I am suggesting that we become "level-blind."

The Macro Level of Serving East

What we have talked about so far is the relationship between you and your external customer at the micro level. Now, let's shoot up to 30,000 feet and look from the macro level of your organization's relationship with its customers.

As the CEO and board look east, they realize that the old ways of measuring customer satisfaction are not going to work anymore. Jill Griffin is an expert on the subject of customer service whom I am fortunate to have gotten to know over the years. I have gone to school on her great book called *Customer Loyalty: How to Earn It, How to Keep It*. In it she makes a compelling case that the way we measure customer satisfaction is antiquated and the tools we use to measure it are unreliable.

Here is what she says is the solution:

> *If customer satisfaction is unreliable, then what measurement is tied to repeat purchase?*
>
> *The measurement is customer loyalty. In the past, efforts to gain customer satisfaction have attempted to influence the attitude of the customer. The concept of customer loyalty is geared more to behavior than to attitude. When a customer is loyal, he or she exhibits purchase behavior defined as nonrandom purchase expressed over time by some decision-making unit. The term nonrandom is key. A loyal customer has a specific bias about what and from whom to buy. His or her purchase is not a random event. In addition, the term loyalty connotes a condition of some duration and requires that the act of purchase occur no less than two times. Finally, the term decision-making unit indicates that the decision to purchase may be made by more than one person. In such a case, a purchase decision can represent a compromise by individuals in the unit and can explain why individuals are sometimes not loyal to their most preferred product or service.[9]*

Customer loyalty can be cultivated. However, referencing my opening example of losing the Dell account, the operations people inside of an organization can make or break us. And to Jill's point

---

9 Jill Griffin, *Customer Loyalty: How to Earn It, How to Keep It* (New York: Lexington Books, 1995), 4.

above, purchase decisions often represent a compromise by a number of stakeholders inside our eastern-vector customers.

As we focus on serving east, we must think about all the stakeholders in the organization, and not just the ones in the greatest perceived positions of power. Why? Well, firstly, the power players can move on to other companies, and their replacements may want to change the relationship. If we have engendered strong customer loyalty throughout the customer organization, that is less likely to happen.

Secondly, our reputation throughout a customer organization can make or break the delivery of our current product or service and can impact future engagements. So, we need to ensure that we are serving the entire customer entity, and not just playing to a select audience, no matter how tempting that seems when we are in the king's chamber.

Thirdly, if we are to achieve customer loyalty, that implies repeat business, where the customer wants to do business with us again. If they do so reluctantly because of a top-down edict, that does not set everyone up for a great, successful relationship. And, if they are doing business with us against their will, or better judgement, that will surely impact our reputation in the marketplace and hurt us down the road.

The Need for Sacrifice

Here is something my very first mentor, Dr. Nicholas Marchese, told me as I was just starting out in my career. This timeless wisdom has helped me help myself and others who have sought to grow to the next level, from the micro of the individual to the macro of a global corporation. He said:

Maturity is sacrificing present gains for future goals.

As you know, the present gain of immediate gratification for accomplishing a result with a customer can be seen as a somewhat immature approach to customer service. We have to take the long view if we want our customers to become loyal to us. Beyond simple customer satisfaction in the moment, we want a relationship that stands the test of time. A mature external customer service approach will often involve making extremely hard calls over tradeoffs. Of course, this is why you, the leader, get paid a lot more than frontline employees—to make those hard calls.

East-West Highway

Just as we saw that there is a distinct north-south highway that needs to be successfully navigated, so too is there a major east-west thoroughfare that requires continual maintenance. Just like a highway, if left unattended and unmaintained, the road will go from great to terrible in short order. To further our metaphor, there are not unlimited resources to maintain a highway. Good planning has to occur so that limited resources can be applied where most needed, and there are always tradeoffs.

In very difficult tradeoffs, choices are often painful and have negative consequences no matter what. Trying to keep everyone happy, north, south, east and west, can be a nightmare at worst, and like playing Whac-a-Mole at best. Yes, it is really tough. But because you are a leader, you suck it up, put on your ODD hat, and go to work.

ODD

As a leader, whether you know it or not, you are engaged in ODD behavior at all times. OD = organizational development; OD also = organizational design. OD is the science of planned change— change management, if you will. Most universities have Ph.D. programs in OD, but if you talk to someone with a Ph.D. in OD, they will fall on one side of the equation or the other. Organizational development is skewed toward developing the people, whereas organizational design is skewed more toward the systems. Therefore, I call it ODD.

My belief is that as a leader, you need to be adept at running your own ODD initiatives and should avoid relying on external change agents (OD consultants). And I believe you are already following this advice. You may not realize you are doing ODD initiatives, but you are. It is important to realize that you are performing change management, as this will help you be more intentional about the process.

As you work on your east-west customer journey, you have ODD tools at your disposal. Which type of OD you use depends on the situation. Sometimes, you work on the systems first, and the development of the people and teams will follow. Sometimes you work on the people side of the equation first, because you already have good systems in place, and you just need people to follow your well-designed systems.

No Silver Bullets

Making your east-west journey smooth for everyone is a difficult objective to achieve. Your job is one with many stakeholders, often with competing demands. So, I am not offering a silver bullet or panacea. What I am suggesting is that the topic of satisfying our external customers while keeping our internal customers satisfied as well needs to be continually wrestled with. There is more to the customer journey than "their" journey; both our internal customer journey and external customer journey must have clear navigation and smooth roads with few potholes. In short, the east-west highway needs to be super smooth for maximum speed. And your customer compass tells you there are four distinct vectors to consider.

What I can offer in terms of solutions are some ideas:

1. East-west challenges must be addressed and transparently discussed up and down the food chain. There should be open dialogue at every level, and upper management needs to listen and wrestle with the inevitable tradeoffs.

2. If we come from a place of genuine desire to serve our customers, both internal and external, it will show through, and compromises will be made without individuals or groups taking the decisions personally.

3. It is important to realize we will generally not be able to please everyone and make all stakeholders happy. But as another mentor of mine has said, "Happiness is overrated." Our customers may not always be happy, but will they be loyal? That is the question. Personally, I believe that you can have both. It is often the degree and frequency of the unhappiness that will determine the ability for a given stakeholder to be loyal, be it an internal or external one.

4. Attitude is everything. Jill Griffin will help me make this point with another excerpt from Customer Loyalty:

   Having a "system to run on" is important for building loyalty; procedures, guidelines, tracking systems, and communication material are important tools that help employees perform. But that's just part of the equation. The real success of your loyalty system is not just in having the right tools but in having those tools used by employees with loyalty-driven attitudes. Says Tommaso Zanzotto, American Express travel president, "When you want to increase customer satisfaction, technical training—how to write a letter to a card member, for example—is easy. The quantum leap comes from improving employees' attitudes." When this attitude is not present, even the best-conceived system can break down.[10]

---

10 Griffin, *Customer Loyalty*, 220-221.

I am sure this list of ideas is far from complete, and that you have many great ideas on how to ensure the east-west highway is a smoother ride for your customers.

What are your thoughts? May I suggest you make a list and share it with your leader and your colleagues? You are all in this together and want to make the customer experience a great one, for all stakeholders, no matter what their vector.

Solving East-Facing Problems

As you face east, what are the problems you are trying to solve with your external customers? Each company has its own relatively unique set of challenges with external customers. And each organization within each company has a different set of challenges to varying degrees. Here are some ideas for solving your customer problems, from the macro of the company to the micro at the individual level. They are very basic, and you are invariably already doing them, but they are worth mentioning:

1. Recognize that there are problems. Denial is sweet, but also deadly when it comes to our eastern vector.

2. Assess where the problems are; assess the severity of the issue; prioritize.

3. Openly look at them; bring them into the full light of day; make them fully visible to all internal stakeholders.

4. Actively discuss how to solve them.

Item number four brings up the idea of IDS, championed by Gino Wickman, author of Traction: Get a Grip on Your Business.

> *Clearly identify the real issue, because the stated problem is rarely the real one. The underlying issue is always a few layers down. Most of the time, the stated problem is a symptom of the real issue, so that you must find the root*

of the matter. By batting the issue back and forth, you will reach the true cause.

Plan on getting a little bit uncomfortable. Most causes of real issues are people. The discussion can hit close to home if either someone on the leadership team or one of his or her staff is responsible. You have to be able to talk about the elephant in the room. That is why trust is so important. You have to become more vulnerable with each other and be willing to be straight about the real problems. Remember the greater good.[11]

IDS

Last year, a private equity firm hired me to install Traction, an organizational operating system, inside of their management firm and in all their portfolio companies. As I was facilitating one of the meetings where we were learning the IDS system, Scott Friesen, Chairman of the Board, was struggling through a big issue. He and his team were coming up with all kinds of solutions to the presenting problem—underscore "presenting." It only took a slight nudge for them to move deeper.

"Scott, the 'I' of IDS does not mean 'identify.' It stands for 'identify root cause.' "

Scott's eyes lit up. "Yes, that's right." He asked his team, "What is the root cause of this problem?"

Fifteen minutes later, the executive leadership team had dug down to the reason below the reason for the problem, identified the root cause, and solved the issue. Instead of solving the symptom, they solved the causal agent, and the problem has never resurfaced.

As Gino stated, the presenting problem is rarely the root cause.

---

11 Gino Wickman, Traction: *Get a Grip on Your Business* (Dallas, TX: BenBella Books, Inc., 2011), 137.

Dig down deep when you are trying to solve these complex east-west issues. Ask yourself, "What is the root cause of the problem?" Identifying the root cause is often half the battle.

Continuous Improvement

The east-west corridor is mission-critical for an organization's success. Those who say they have no customer issues have blind spots and are mistaken. And while perhaps the problems they do have are minor and insignificant right now, customer satisfaction and loyalty are like the Texas weather ... just wait a little while and you will have a new forecast.

To continue with this metaphor a little further, how is the weather on your east-west roadway? Is your road in great condition and traffic flowing freely in both directions, or do you have some issues like those below?

- Blizzard Whiteout
- Bumper to Bumper Traffic
- Construction Detour
- Bridge Washed Out
- Fog Causing Poor Visibility

If the relationship between east and west required road signs, which ones would you choose?

- Slippery When Wet
- Road Closed
- Beware of Curves
- Animal Crossing
- Slow Down
- Minimum Speed 60 MPH
- Sharp Turn Ahead

- Danger

- Merge Left

- Workers Ahead

- School Zone

In summary, what can you do to make sure that this east-west road is a sleek eight-lane superhighway? We will wrap up this section by letting Jill help make the final point.

> *Just like the world we live in, your loyalty system must be ever changing. The particular methods you employ to earn loyalty today may need a major overhaul twelve months from now. You must keep modifying, upgrading, and changing your system to meet the changing demands of your marketplace and your customer. As we have seen, there are no loyalty guarantees. Unless you continue to provide value, as your customers define it, even your most seemingly loyal customers and clients will eventually go elsewhere. … But as we pointed out, everything changes … Start right now to devise new ways to get and keep your customers … loyalty is developed and earned one step at a time.*[12]

To drive this metaphor through the floor, we could talk about toll roads. In order for them to be successful, they have to get us where we are going easier, faster, and/or better than the non-toll route. If it is painful to take a toll road, then we won't, except as a last resort. And when a better route becomes available, we will take that instead. Making our customer's journey as pleasant as possible at all levels of our organization, in both directions, is really our ultimate goal.

---

12 Griffin, Customer Loyalty, 228.

Recap

Now, let's recap where we have been in this chapter. Traveling from the micro to the macro level:

- At the individual level, I demonstrated what not to emulate: the arrogance of the top-down leader who does not have time for "low-level" people.

- We discussed how people at all levels of an organization can make or break a customer relationship, and why it is critical that you, the leader, have the right mentality when dealing with external customers.

- We also spoke about how it is essential that you develop your staff and cascade a positive customer service attitude throughout your organization, right to frontline employees.

- We addressed stakeholders, both internal and external, and how keeping everyone satisfied is a very difficult job, which is why you get paid the big bucks to do the best to make that happen.

- At the 30,000-foot macro-view of the customer, from the office of the CEO and senior team, we saw how customer service is not enough, and that we need to drive to customer loyalty, which is a step change beyond having a satisfied external customer.

- Finally, we saw that this east-west set of relationships is critical to your organizational health and the healthy relationship with internal and external customers.

Where do we go from here?

What is missing in a discussion of your eastern vector?

You might ask, "Daniel, what about the impossible employees inside of our customer companies? How do we deal with them?" Or you may ask, "What about the impossible employees inside of our company, who are terrible at customer service? What do we do about them?"

Great questions. This brings us to the topic of employee health and employee temperament. A short while ago, we read a quote from Tommaso Zanzotto discussing employee attitude. While I think this is certainly important, what I am talking about goes beyond the attitudes of your employees or those of your external customers.

Employee Health

One of the biggest factors in effective customer service, north, south, east, and west, is the health of the individual and the quality of the interactions between individuals. After all, at the end of the day, it is all about the people and how they interact with each other and our systems. Therefore, individual health really matters.

I opened this chapter with my own personal story. What you saw was a snapshot of a person who was sick both physically and emotionally. My dependence on alcohol as a crutch for dealing with pressure put me at a great disadvantage when I was dealing with an external customer. It was also damaging for those who worked with me. You can't give someone your best when you are hung over.

Your employees run the gamut from physically very healthy to physically very sick. On the unhealthy side, some may be dealing with any number of addictions: food, work, substances, approval, and more. Some may be dealing with physical maladies from the relatively innocuous flu to the profound game changers like heart disease and cancer.

Emotional Health

On the emotional health side, your employees also are on the continuum of very emotionally healthy to very emotionally unhealthy. As an alcoholic and a workaholic, I was unhealthy on both accounts. Emotionally, I was selfish and self-centered, the antithesis of a servant leader. Physically, I was self-medicating to handle stress. Both were maladaptive and deleterious to my wellbeing and that of my internal and external customers.

There came a point when I had to make a choice. Doug McCullough, a client, gave me the Big Book of Alcoholics Anonymous. Without Doug's willingness to point out my problem, I might have stayed in denial for who knows how long. Instead, I have enjoyed over twenty-four years of freedom from the "ism" that drove me to drink too much and work too hard.

As a people manager, you are dealing with employee health issues all day long. If you are the type of leader who truly cares about your employees, you are also likely sensitive to all that I am saying, and regularly probe into people's state of mental and physical wellbeing. Asking "How are you doing?" really does not cut it. Our instinctive response when asked is to say, "Fine. I'm just fine." The truth is that sometimes there is a raging fire going on within that person, or their family. So too with your external customers.

We never really know the depths of what is going on inside someone else's world, but we can certainly strive to find out. First, we have to give a flip.

Assumptions Are Dangerous

Steven Covey, famous author of many leadership books, including *The 7 Habits of Highly Effective People*, told a story once of his time riding a subway in my hometown, New York City.

As Stephen got on the train and sat down, he began looking around, checking out the people in the subway car. He noticed the man directly across from him was slouched over, with his head in his hands. What appeared to be his two young children were running up and down the car, yelling and carrying on as if they were in a playground.

Stephen grew perturbed. "That is not a very good parent," he thought. "He has no discipline over his children." The children kept up the commotion, stop after stop, and the man seemed to not even notice. Finally, Stephen had enough and could contain himself no longer. He leaned across the aisle and blurted out, "Sir, can't you control your children?"

The man looked up sadly and said, "I am sorry. We are just coming from the hospital, where we just lost their mother. I guess this is their way of dealing with it."

Ouch.

Empathy Is Key

We never know what someone else is going through, what they are struggling with, or how we can be helpful until we ask—and usually, probe further. This takes a certain amount of courage.

Here is a technique you can use to break beyond the instinctive response of "I'm fine." If you ask how someone is, and they say "Fine," you say some variation on the theme of, "Tell me how you are really doing." You may add, "I care, and truly want to know." Obviously, you should not use this technique if you don't care. And if you don't care, I would question if you should be in a people leadership role.

I would like to bring in a few experts to join me in further exploring this subject of employee health. Before I do that, let me remind you why this is so important. If you have an unhealthy person talking to your customers, that often produces unhealthy relationships. This is true on both sides. What makes life even more interesting is when you have two unhealthy employees on each side of the east-west equation. Fun.

I have a client right now who has just joined a company where he has to work with a very sick colleague. I am not a doctor, so I cannot diagnose him, but he has all the classic signs of a full-blown case of narcissistic personality disorder. That is the single most common issue after clinical depression that I see in the senior leadership of organizations. Why that is I will save for another day. The fact that it has to be dealt with and worked around is certainly a huge issue. Everyone is walking on eggshells around this person for fear of upsetting him in some small way and experiencing intense, venomous anger and personal attacks. Clearly, a very unhealthy situation.

I have another situation where the external customer of my client is a control freak, and it is an almost impossible situation for my client company. They can't fire their biggest client, but this person is so difficult to deal with, they are the subject of countless management team meetings. And I am sure many people have a picture of this person on their dartboard.

There are physically and emotionally unhealthy employees in all directions. You, the leader, need to be adept at identifying and navigating these issues.

How do you do that? Here are three quick suggestions—I am sure you can think of many more:

1. Recognize that in any given organization you are going to have a certain percentage of mental issues. According to the US National Institute of Mental Health, almost one in five people have some type of mental illness.

2. Take classes to improve your awareness of people and what makes them tick. For example, become a student of the behavioral sciences; the DISC model is a great place to start.

3. Study emotional intelligence. A great book on the subject (there are many) is *Emotional Intelligence 2.0* by Travis Bradberry and Jean Greaves. It has a nifty online assessment included when you buy the book, and it can help you and your team improve awareness.

Pertaining to point #3 above, think about this:

No matter whether people measure high or low in EQ, they can work to improve it, and those who score low can actually catch up to their coworkers. Research conducted at the business school at the University of Queensland in Australia discovered that people who are low in EQ and job performance can match their colleagues who excel in both—solely by working to improve their EQ.

Of all the people we've studied at work, we have found that 90 percent of high performers are also high in EQ. On the flip side, just 20 percent of low performers are high in EQ. You can be a high performer without EQ, but the chances are slim. People who develop their EQ tend to be successful on the job because the two go hand in hand. Naturally, people with high EQs make more money—an average of $29,000 more per year than people with low EQs. The link between EQ and earnings is so direct that every point increase in EQ adds $1,300 in annual salary.[13]

---

13 Travis Bradberry and Jean Greaves, *Emotional Intelligence 2.0* (San Diego: TalentSmart, 2009), 21.

Starting with Self

The easiest and hardest place to start with a discussion about employee health is with you. Looking in the mirror can be painful. We would like to see ourselves with many strengths and few weaknesses. But you must take a hard look if you are going to use your customer compass for maximum effectiveness. You may be reluctant to look at some weaknesses, or if you are like me, have been working on the same character defect (patience) for decades, with only marginal results. You may feel like giving up. Or you may feel like you are done. Let me encourage you. Wherever you are on your journey, the 1,000-mile walk begins with the first step. Don't give up. Persevere. The journey to next-level leadership is worth it. You are worth it. You can do it. Get your head straight, stand up, and put one foot in front of the other. One day at a time. Before long, you will see how far you have come. And it's not like you are just starting out on your journey. You have been at this for decades already. You likely know where your weak points are. If you don't, just ask your significant other. They are always ready to help in this area.

Maybe you need to mature as a leader. I certainly do. Let me offer some helpful thinking along this line from Ryan Holiday and his book, *Ego Is the Enemy*.

> *In most cases, we think that people become successful through sheer energy and enthusiasm. We almost excuse ego because we think it's part and parcel of the personality required to "make it big." Maybe a bit of that overpowering-ness is what got you where you are. But let's ask: Is it really sustainable for the next several decades? Can you really out-work and outrun everyone forever? The answer is no. The ego tells us we're invincible, that we have unlimited force that will never dissipate. But that can't be what greatness requires—energy without end? ... Yet the rest of*

us want to get to the top as fast as humanly possible. We have no patience for waiting. We're high on getting high up the ranks. Once we've made it, we tend to think that ego and energy is the only way to stay there. It's not.[14]

Ryan goes on to talk about the "sobriety" of humility, which is the enemy of the ego.

Ego Is My Enemy

I don't know about you, but my ego gets me in trouble from time to time. How does this relate to serving our customers to the east? Well, our ego usually is trying to prove itself "right" and the other person "wrong."

Like Covey, we can make assumptions about what is going on in a customer's world and ascribe motives to their actions. I used to do that all the time, and really had to work on breaking myself from that bad habit. I can't possibly know what someone else's motives are without a deep dive into their psyche. And I am usually moving too fast to take that kind of time.

So, I have a choice. I can either slow down and do that deep dive, learning what makes that crazy, difficult-to-deal-with customer tick, or I can simply take what is going on at face value, observing the actions but avoiding judging that person. If I make such assumptions as, "She is trying to sabotage my project," or, "He enjoys trying to make my life difficult," or any other story I could come up with in my head as to why someone is acting the way they are, I would likely be dead wrong. I can quickly find myself acting on wrong information I made up in my head, and the next thing you know—conflict of some sort occurs.

---

14 Ryan Holiday, *Ego Is the Enemy* (New York: Portfolio / Penguin, 2016), 145.

Fighting for Fair

In dealing with customers, we often think of what is fair or not fair. This is dangerous ground when we are assessing something that is affecting us personally. I will let Ryan continue to help us here:

> *Ego loves the notion, the idea that something is "fair" or not. Psychologists call it narcissistic injury when we take personally totally indifferent and objective events. We do that when our sense of self is fragile and dependent on life going our way all the time. Whether what you're going through is your fault or your problem doesn't matter, because it's yours to deal with right now. ... Humble and strong people don't have the same trouble with these troubles that egotists do. There are fewer complaints and far less self-immolation. Instead, there's stoic—even cheerful—resilience. Pity isn't necessary. Their identity isn't threatened. They can get by without constant validation. This is what we're aspiring to—much more than mere success. What matters is that we can respond to what life throws at us. And how we make it through.[15]*

By now, you may be thinking, *This is going in a way different direction than I thought. What does this have to do with customer service?* Worse, you might be thinking I played a dirty trick to get you this far, only to have you start taking a hard look at yourself.

Why have we gone here? Because you are critical to any kind of customer service, north, south, east, or west. Any direction you turn, the one constant is you. How you interface with these vectors determines the quality of the customer service your customer receives from you. Will it be an ego-based interface? Or will it be one that is not about you, but about your genuine, authentic desire to serve your customer, wherever they are, and in whatever kind

---

15 Holiday, *Ego Is the Enemy,* 167-169.

of emotional or physical health?

Further, you have to translate this idea of "ego is the enemy" to your customers to the west and the south. You can't give what you haven't got, so getting your own ego out of the way is the first step. Next, translate clear messaging to others that we can't let our ego get in the way of serving our customers to the east.

Self-Esteem vs. Ego

Over the years of working with leaders, I have noticed a fascinating phenomenon. To explain this, I first need you to see a continuum with high ego on the far left and high self-esteem on the far right. Plot yourself somewhere along that line. Where do you think you are? What I have noticed is that those with very high ego as their internal operating system invariably have low self-esteem, and they are using ego to mask the issue. Conversely, those with high self-esteem have low ego. They operate by having a strong sense of self, without having an ego that needs accolades or affirmation.

Would it be useful for you to ponder where you are on this continuum?

EGO |————————————————| **SELF-ESTEEM**

What does self-esteem have to do with delivering great customer service? The higher the self-esteem, the better you will be able to navigate difficult customer interactions in any vector, without taking issues personally. You will be better able to remain objective, calm, and centered, and respond from a place of true caring to meet that customer's needs without your ego getting in the way. And when your ego does get in the way (as it will—no one is perfect), and you cause some kind of upset, your high self-esteem enables you to apologize to the customer without your ego being bruised or threatened.

You can "clean your side of the street," so to speak. You will avoid making the customer wrong for not cleaning theirs (and apologizing). You will move on to solving the problem by de-escalating the conflict. You will be an internal hero. You will swallow your pride and come out a winner.

High self-esteem also enables you to deal with the unhealthy people you work with, north, south, east, and west. And believe me, they don't know who they are. They are walking around breaking all kinds of glass and are often relatively clueless as to why they are experiencing such a difficult time at work. You can better navigate these crazy situations if your ego is in check and your self-esteem high.

Have I lost you? I think so. Your mind has wandered to that truly insane customer who genuinely needs a month of rest in a padded cell somewhere safe. Dealing with these folks is another reason you get paid the big bucks.

Source of Self-Esteem

I assume you are asking yourself, "Where does self-esteem come from, and how can it be raised?" Great question. We don't have time for more than but a quick mention, and I am really not trying to be a wise guy when I say this: Self-esteem is the esteem you give yourself. Therefore, give yourself more esteem. Ah, if it were only that easy.

Notice the title of this section. It is singular. You are the source. Only you. It is not outside of you. You are the creator of it, and can raise it or lower it, simply by your actions. *How do you do that?* you may wonder. Read on.

Self-Talk

To grow your self-esteem, you have to control your self-talk. The talk you tell yourself. You are constantly sending yourself mental messages. Some are innocuous. Some are profound. The profound ones really matter and have a huge impact on performance.

Nathaniel Branden wrote a classic on the subject: *Self-Esteem at Work: How Confident People Make Powerful Companies*.

In it he writes:

> *Self-esteem pertains to an experience of efficacy. This entails confidence in your mind at a very deep level. Not the confidence of knowing you can perform this or that task appropriately. Not confidence in how much you may know about any particular subject. Rather, it means trust in the processes by which you reason, understand, learn, choose, decide, and regulate action. It is a trust that cannot be faked. It has to be reality-based—has to be earned.[16]*

For those who struggle with low to moderate self-esteem, I encourage you to read this book. Nathaniel will show you how to "earn" your self-esteem.

Imagine two golfers of the exact same skill and ability, playing each other. One gets up to tee off, and his self-talk—the thoughts running through his head—is *I am probably going to shank the ball and lose it in the trees.* His opponent's thought as she is teeing off is, *I am going to hit the ball long and straight.* Who is going to win that tournament? You're right, the woman, who has the better self-talk.

---

16 Nathaniel Branden, *Self-Esteem at Work: How Confident People Make Powerful Companies* (San Francisco: Jossey-Bass, 1998), ix.

Feed the Right Dog

This reminds me of a quick story. There is a guy who races dogs for a living. He has two greyhounds, a white one and a black one. He goes to the racetrack every week, runs both dogs, bets on only one of them, and always wins. It is completely uncanny.

One week, he races both dogs, bets on the white one, and sure enough, the white one wins. The next week, he races both dogs, bets on the black one, and like clockwork, the black one wins. When interviewed by the press, demanding to know the secret to his success, he nonchalantly replies, "That's easy. I just bet on the dog I am feeding that week."Please do not think this is anything less than a profound truth. The dog you feed will win.

Are you feeding the dog of negativity?

Do you allow negative thoughts about your own performance?

Do you talk to yourself in ways that are less than encouraging and edifying?

Would you allow others to talk to you the way you talk to yourself?

If you are your own worst critic, and you are constantly beating yourself up, you are hurting your self-esteem. If you have always done this and think it is your secret sauce for getting to the next level, I will echo the words of my friend Marshall Goldsmith by reading to you the title of his incredible book: "What got you here won't get you there."

In one of my favorite skits, Bob Newhart plays a psychiatrist. His patient is going on and on and on about her problem. Bob finally leans over the desk and says in a hushed tone: "Would you like me to tell you how to get better?" The patient says *"Yes, please!"* Bob leans back over the desk and loudly yells, *"Then, stop it!"* Startled, the patient pauses a moment, and then goes back into a diatribe on the problem. Once again, the patient is asked if she wants the cure. Once again, the patient enthusiastically says *"Yes."* Once again, this time even louder, Shrink Bob yells *"Just stop it!"* This goes on until you just want to reach into the TV and yell at the patient yourself. Are you in the problem, mired in your negative self-talk? Are you saying things like, *"This is all good in theory, but this would never work for me"*? Or *"This would never work in our company"*? Control your self-talk and you will become a better leader, guaranteed.

Feeding the Right People

Now, let's take the focus off of you and shine it on your people. Speaking of feeding—some of them you might want to stop feeding, figuratively speaking. Let's listen to Marshall:

> *In the same way some of your problems do not need fixing because they are an issue to only a small minority of people. As a boss you should stop trying to change people who don't want to change. This may sound harsh, but some people are unsalvageable. You're only banging your head against a wall if you think you can fix them.*[17]

Marshall then goes on to list the types you should help find a job opportunity outside your company.

Namely:

- People who don't think they have a problem.

- People who are pursuing the wrong strategy for the organization.

- People who should not be in their job; they are not qualified for whatever reason.

- People who think everyone else is the problem.

---

17 Marshall Goldsmith, *What Got You Here Won't Get You There: How Successful People Become Even More Successful* (New York: Hachette Books, 2014), 218.

As a leader, your job is to be healthy, develop healthy employees, and in the spirit of this book, teach them how to best serve customers, north, south, east, and west. It is also your job to exit those who are not right for your organization.

We focused on you first, because to quote a wise saying I once heard, "You can't give someone something you don't have." So, we had to first make sure your attitude was right.

Now, we can start working on your people. However, instead of pages more of "how to develop your people," allow me to refer you to Chapter 2: South, where we addressed that already.

A Critical Job

As we discussed previously, one of your main jobs is to be a great coach, trainer, mentor, and developer of your direct reports.

What I have repeatedly heard, read and seen over the course of my executive coaching career is that developing direct reports should take up between 20 and 25% of an executive's job, and that executives tend to spend nowhere near that percentage of their time on it. The tendency is to over-index on task and project management—getting stuff done—and under-index on people development—growing your people to the next level of effectiveness.

If this is you, don't beat yourself up for this being the case. Just start now to be more intentional in the growing of your direct reports, and consciously show them that they, too, have a customer compass in their pocket or on their dashboard—whatever visual works best. My car has a rear-view mirror. On it, my onboard compass gives a readout of my heading. When I pay attention to it, I am better oriented directionally.

Help your people to think in terms of the four main vectors and orient themselves directionally.

Help them discover answers to these questions:

- Who are my customers to the north?

- Whom am I here to serve to the south?

- Whom to my east do I have to do a better job serving?

- With whom to my west do I need to build a better relationship?

Help your direct reports to get, maintain, and grow their 360-degree view of the customer. Help them to see their role is that of serving customers. How? By creating a customer service–centric culture.

Serving Two Masters

Once you start broaching this 360-degree view of serving customers with your direct reports and colleagues, you are sure to meet resistance. Some will say it can't be done—that you can't serve two masters. What do you think? Can you effectively serve external customers **and** internal stakeholders? If your answer is "no," then I would say you have given up and you need to step down from a leadership role.

Is this a very difficult job? You bet.

We already agreed that this is super hard.Will it take constant work? Absolutely.

Is it necessary?

It is not only necessary, but also essential.

Can the Transportation Department look at road maintenance as optional? Absolutely not. Are there tradeoffs and budgetary constraints? You bet. But not doing anything results in total decay of the roadway and ensuing chaos at rush hour. You may be saying where you live, they have given up on your roads—ha ha!

Come down to Panama City, Panama, where I have my second home, and I will show you what it means to "give up." Our potholes swallow cars whole.The point is that you have to do both. You can't give up. And, you definitely can make a huge difference, with intentionality, determination, and a quick hand at Whac-a-Mole. Is it difficult? Definitely. Is it worth it? You bet.

For Further Discussion

- Have you ever crashed and burned with a customer as a result of your ego? What happened? What lesson(s) did you learn?

- What are some of the tradeoffs you will have to make to serve your external customers while keeping your internal customers happy?

- How can you better serve your existing external customers?

- How can you lead your organization in improving the level of east-bound service?

- What do you think about the concept of the east-west thoroughfare? Do you have great communication going on in both directions? If not, what can you personally do to improve it?

CHAPTER **4**

WEST

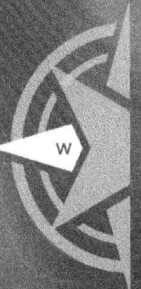

Chapter 4: WEST

Turning your attention west, you see peers, colleagues, and other departments. This is the one vector where we can anticipate some difficulty.

After some reflection on the question of "Who is my customer?" you might say, "Well, I can agree that I need to make my north vector's jobs easier. And certainly, I am here to take care of my southern vector. So, north and south, I can see how those are customers I am here to serve. East is a no-brainer. No paradigm shift required there. But to my west, that is where I have the problem. In fact, I am actually THEIR customer! They are here to serve me. And you know what, they don't do a very good job of it!"

You are likely thinking of an individual in your western vector who is a real pain in the butt. Funny thing to wonder, what if everyone in your western vector were reading this? Who would say that about you?

Recently, I had this very conversation discussing our customer compass model, and was presented with this dilemma: "If your peers in other organizations really should be seeing you as their customer, how can you possibly be delivering customer service to them?" It is a great question.

Let's explore some possible answers and solutions to this dilemma by looking east. Sally, a pretend customer of yours, will help us see one solution.

Introducing Level 5 Leadership

Sally is getting more irritated by the minute. As COO of one of your customers, she has been sitting for an hour in a meeting with her team.

Around the table, she is letting her people vent. They are not happy with how difficult it is to do business with you and your company. "Our operations people are complaining to us all the time," they whine. "Their people are so difficult to do business with, and their process is so rigid." Complaint after complaint with no solution in sight; there is an overwhelming sense of angst in the meeting.

Sally, a Level 5 leader, finally interrupts. "Folks, I am hearing you wallow in your problem. What I don't hear is the solution. What are we going to *do* about this?"

This quickly re-focuses the meeting. Her people start brainstorming punitive measures they could take against you and your company. "We can escalate this inside their organization to the senior executives," someone suggests. Everyone except Sally agrees.

"I will take this under advisement," she says, "but I am not convinced that this is the best solution. I will sleep on it and make a decision in the morning. Thank you everyone for your input. Meeting adjourned."

Does this sound familiar? Maybe not, because the last time you were in a customer's meeting where you were the hot topic of conversation was, maybe, never. Sure, you "receive" customer complaints and escalations. But when was the last time you were in on the planning stage, as the escalation was being formulated? This has probably not happened, and understandably so. You are not your customer's employee, and you are not invited behind the curtain to their private conversations about your organization's servicing of their account.

The next day, Sally picks up the phone and calls Barry, the senior vice president over your division. "Barry, we have a problem," she begins.

Barry braces himself. He thinks, *Oh no, not another escalation. Here we go again.*

Sally continues, "Barry, we have not been the best customer we can be for you, and I would like to talk about how we can be better at partnering with your organization to make our relationship work better, at all levels, especially with our frontline and mid-management operations interface."

Wow, Barry thinks. *This is a first.* "So, what I am hearing you say is that you want to better partner with us, Sally. Well, that is very thoughtful of you," he says, and lets out a sigh of relief. "Sure. That would be great. Where can we begin?"

Sally, a Level 5 leader, wins the day for her company, you don't get punished, and soon your two organizations are attempting to partner in making things work better. Her people are over on your side of the equation, brainstorming with your people on improving the problems that have plagued the relationship.

How did Sally do it? Was this a result of her being a Level 5 leader? If so, what is Level 5 leadership, and how could we apply this internally as we explore what it means to our relationships with departments to our west, and this east-west corridor?

Level 5 Leadership Defined

First, about Level 5 leadership. Enter Jim Collins, author of one of the best business books of all time, a must-read and must-have for your library: *Good to Great.* In order to write *Good to Great,* Jim analyzed 1,435 companies and their performance track record over a forty-year period.

The goal of this analysis was to identify those that had been good performers for a long period of time, but then had a transformational series of events that changed them into truly great companies. The metaphor I think of is a caterpillar into a butterfly—without the possibility of going back into the caterpillar state, the butterfly keeps flying high.

Jim looked for a significant period of sustained greatness. He and his large team of researchers were only able to identify eleven companies that transformed from good to great. The purpose of this research project and the subsequent book was to capture the factors that made these eleven companies so successful in their transformation. Wikipedia has this information on the book:

> Good to Great: Why Some Companies Make the Leap... and Others Don't *is a management book by Jim C. Collins that describes how companies transition from being good companies to great companies, and how most companies fail to make the transition. The book was a bestseller, selling four million copies and going far beyond the traditional audience of business books.*[18]

> *"Greatness" is defined by Collins by a company that achieves financial performance several multiples better than the market average, over a sustained period.*

> *Collins and his research team identified a set of elite companies that had made the transition from good to great - and sustained that performance for at least fifteen years.*

> *After the leap, the good-to-great companies generated cumulative stock returns that beat the general stock market by an average of seven times in fifteen years, better than twice the results delivered by a composite index of the world's greatest companies, including Coca-Cola, Intel, General Electric, and Merck. Collins used a large team of researchers who studied "6,000 articles, generated more than 2,000 pages of interview transcripts and created 384 megabytes of computer data in a five-year project."*[19] [20]

18 Adam Bryant, *"For This Guru, No Question Is Too Big,"* New York Times, May 23, 2009, https://www.nytimes.com/2009/05/24/business/24collins.html.

19 "Nonfiction Book Review: *GOOD TO GREAT: Why Some Companies Make the Leap... And Others Don't,"* Publishers Weekly, last modified September 3, 2001, https://www.publishersweekly.com/978-0-06-662099-2.

20 *"Good to Great,"* Wikipedia, Wikimedia Foundation, Inc., last modified October 29,

However, all that is not the point of bringing up this book. What Jim and his team discovered along the way is the point—a phenomenon that he named "the Level 5 leader."

Level 5:
The Executive

Level 4: Effective Leader

Level 3: Competent Manager

Level 2: Contributing Team Member

Level 1: Highly Capable Individual

Jim Collins will explain his model the best:

> *Level 5 leaders channel their ego needs away from themselves and into the larger goal of building a great company. It's not that Level 5 leaders have no ego or self-interest. Indeed, they are incredibly ambitious—but their ambition is first and foremost for the institution, not themselves.*[21]

Jim goes on to write how he discovered the Level 5 leader phenomenon:

> *The term Level 5 refers to the highest level in a hierarchy of executive capabilities that we identified in our research. While you don't need to move in sequence from Level 1 to Level 5—it might be possible to fill in some of the lower levels later—fully developed Level 5 leaders*

2020, https://en.wikipedia.org/wiki/Good_to_Great.
21 Jim Collins, *Good to Great: Why Some Companies Make the Leap... and Others Don't* (New York: HarperCollins, 2001), 21.

embody all five layers of the pyramid. I am not going to belabor all five levels here, as Levels 1 through 4 are somewhat self-explanatory and are discussed extensively by other authors. This chapter will focus instead on the distinguishing traits of the good-to-great leaders—namely Level 5 traits—in contrast to the comparison leaders in our study.[22]

Jim was not looking for a new model of leadership, but the data was compelling. Every one of these eleven companies had a Level 5 leader at the helm during their metamorphosis from a caterpillar into a butterfly. He goes on to explain the critical ingredients of a Level 5 leader, starting with this simple equation:

Humility + Will = Level 5.[23]

This reminds me of Don Stoops, whom I referenced in the introduction, and his saying worth remembering: "Humility is power, under control." My addition is Level 5 humility is great power under great control. Jim continues:

Level 5 leaders are a study in duality: modest and willful, humble and fearless ... in contrast to the very I-centric style of the comparison leaders, we were struck by how the good-to-great leaders didn't talk about themselves. During interviews ... they'd talk about the company and the contribution of other executives as long as we'd like but would deflect discussion about their own contributions. ... It wasn't just false modesty. Those who worked with or wrote about the good-to-great leaders continually used words like quiet, humble, modest, reserved, shy, gracious, mild-mannered, self-effacing, understated, did not believe his own clippings; and so forth.[24]

---

22 Collins, *Good to Great*, 22.
23 Collins, *Good to Great*, 22.
24 Collins, *Good to Great*, 27.

Jim makes it clear that humility is only 50% of the equation. He writes:

> *It is very important to grasp that Level 5 leadership is not just about humility and modesty. It is equally about ferocious resolve, an almost stoic determination to do whatever needs to be done to make the company great. Indeed, we debated for a long time on the research team about how to describe the good-to-great leaders. Initially, we penciled in terms like "selfless executive" and "servant leader." But members of the team violently objected to these characterizations. "Those labels don't ring true," said Anthony Chirikos. "It makes them sound weak or meek, but that's not at all the way I think of Darwin Smith or Colman Mockler. They would do almost anything to make the company great." Level 5 leaders are fanatically driven, infected with an incurable need to produce results.[25]*

Earlier in this book, I said that servant leadership was one model of leadership, and that it was not perfect. Neither is the Level 5 model. However, both are useful as you grow your leadership skills to the next level. Both have a lot to offer. And both have a lot in common. It is most useful to look at the similarities:

- Emphasis on humility.

- Emphasis on serving others in an altruistic way.

- Emphasis on getting results.

Both have a slightly different connotation, and those with a high D or I behavioral style will be more drawn to a Level 5 model, where those with a high S or C behavioral style may be more drawn to a servant-leader model. Reiterating what I said early on, a blended approach that synthesizes these and other leadership models is what I see that works best, practically speaking. And of course,

---

25 Collins, *Good to Great*, 30.

you have to develop your own style of leadership, borrowing from all the great thinkers on the subject.

Which reminds me: What is the difference between plagiarism and leadership? Plagiarism is where you steal one thing from one person, and leadership is where you steal everything from everyone! Freely take the best from all the leadership models out there. Make it your motto to "take the best and leave the rest." No author I have ever read has THE perfect leadership model. You need to synthesize this information here with all other things you have ever learned, and then make it your own.

Before we get distracted with the next logical question, "What other leadership models should I look at?" allow me to deflect and suggest that a simple Google search will answer this question. There are many. For now, let's move on to how Level 5 and servant leadership apply to your western vector.

Level Zero

Before Sally became a Level 5 leader, she was abysmal to work for and with. Sally was a terror on wheels, and she was especially hard on vendors. Yes—that is what she called you—a vendor, and just like a vending machine, she would put her quarters in, press the button, and if the object of her desire did not immediately pop out, some choice words might ensue. That is, until she learned that kicking the machine would drop the goods right where she wanted them. Then, when the vending machine broke due to excessive forced labor, she would vent at the supplier of the vending machine. When they stopped wanting to do business with her, she got a new supplier. She went through a lot of vending machines before she matured as a leader.

As Sally progressed in her career from frontline manager to second-line (director) to a candidate for a third-line (VP) role, she read books on leadership, went to leadership workshops, enrolled in leadership courses, and got a few leadership mentors. Sally realized that what got her to this level did not scale to the next— that *"what got her here wouldn't get her there."* She had to change, and change she did.

As we saw, Sally became a Level 5 leader. Her intense drive to get results did not diminish. Just the opposite. But she became comfortable in her own skin, and stopped trying so hard to prove herself, to look good, to get recognition, to be rewarded, and more.

She became humble. That humility was what enabled her to call Barry, and instead of "kicking the vending machine," she partnered with him in solving his problem. She apologized for being a difficult customer. She asked with complete sincerity, "How can I help you?" and, "How can we better partner together for our mutual success?"

Level 5 West

Now you can see how Level 5 leadership applies to your western colleagues. Your peers are not vendors. They are certainly not coin-operated and will not respond well to being kicked. The very best way you can work with them is by taking a proactive approach to problem-solving. With all the humility you can muster, you may need to apologize to some for being a difficult customer. You may want to express remorse for not attempting to walk in their shoes and see their point of view (having empathy). You may even want to confess that you had ascribed motives to their actions and were taking things personally when you now realize that they were just trying to protect their team, resources, time, and money.

Yes, you are going to be able to see how these colleagues are not very good at Level 5 leadership themselves. It will be painfully obvious to you that such turf protection is a big part of the problem. You will see clearly how these silos need to be torn down. But kicking the vending machine will not work. Treating your partner like a vendor will not work. Partnering with your partner in a humble but intensively company-focused drive for results will.

There is a lot more that can be said about treating your peers in various other departments as customers, partnering with them to find mutual solutions to your common problems. We could talk for a long time about the "how" of partnering—how you are going to effectively "walk a mile in their shoes" to truly understand where they are coming from. But suffice it to say that the attitude of "wanting to" is first and foremost. If you have that, then operationalizing this concept will be relatively easy. Simply start the conversation in a humble way that is not pointing fingers, blaming, or accusing your colleague of any type of malpractice. These would certainly not be recommended techniques to kick off a partnering discussion. This same approach works in every other vector as well.

Level 5 South

How can this same humble approach work to the south? Well, you could apologize to your low performers for not being a very good developer of them. You have failed to invest the time and energy required to really help them get where they need to be—or you have failed to point out where they were not meeting expectations. You are disappointed in yourself and your failure, for now you have let the situation become relatively dire, and there is little time to fix this before a decision has to be made as to whether this will work long-term. But you are going to change your ways, and really start investing the time into helping this low performer improve their performance. And when you have given it your best, and if your expectations are still not being met, you will help this person realize that there has been too much damage done, the relationship is not salvageable, and it is time for them to have a fresh start in a new company. All this as you are apologizing for your failure to develop them into all that they needed to be.

With your high performers, you are celebrating their successes and giving them the spotlight, not taking it for yourself. You have high self-esteem. You know you worked hard behind the scenes to help this employee rise to a place of recognition. But you don't need to be recognized. You know you did a great job developing this person. Your reward is that your people are being recognized for the rock stars you have helped them become.

All this to say that behind the scenes, you are known as absolutely tirelessly working toward hitting the company's objectives for your area of responsibility. You have that phenomenal drive for excellence in all that you do. You are fully aligned with the corporate vision, mission, and values, and have adopted them as your own. Everyone knows you as a results-driven, key-metrics-focused leader who is passionate about serving others while meeting goals. That combination is your reputation.

Level 5 North

To the north, you are apologizing to your boss for not having the regular one-on-ones that you had thought were your leader's responsibility to drive. You state that you now realize it is your responsibility to make those happen, and if one gets cancelled, you will be fastidious about rescheduling (rather than relieved).

You will have the same conversation with your northern mentors. You thought they had to chase you, and you now realize that it is your responsibility to ensure you get regular time with them. You apologize for not being an excellent mentee and ask, "How can I get more out of our mentoring sessions?" You even start asking for homework assignments.

You also realize that the north is your customer, and as such, you have to deliver excellent service. In order to do that, you get on the side of your customer, and walk in their shoes a bit by asking excellent probing questions that enable you to see the work through their eyes, and your performance through their lens. When receiving constructive feedback, instead of getting defensive and explaining context when you feel misunderstood, you say, "Thank you for the feedback. Do you have any other ideas on how I can improve?" You realize your northern customers also need to partner with you, but you are not going to wait for them to make the first move. Boldly and with full confidence, you broach the topic of your performance, asking, "If you could change anything about me to make me the best employee you have, what would you change?" When they give you something, instead of getting defensive, you simply say, "Good, what else?"

Level 5 East

To the east, you are apologizing to your customers for not being a better partner. You may apologize to even the truly abusive ones for allowing them to treat you like a vendor, because you know that relationship will not work. No, you need to partner with them to solve their problems. Together, you can solve anything. Alone, you are not very valuable as a leader. You clearly communicate your desire to reset the relationship and to help solve the tough issues you face. You may even apologize for your failure to effectively partner as you terminate your customer relationship, citing your clear inability to meet their needs. There is a humility in all that you do and say, but right along with that humility is an equally tremendous, powerful focus on driving results for the good of the company.

The Power of Feedback

In all four vectors, there is a common theme: your intense drive to do right by the company and get results, coupled with a humility and meekness we don't normally think of when we view managerial functioning. The key is to stay humble, and a primary way to do that is through feedback. Let's bring in the world's greatest coach again, Marshall Goldsmith, and see what he has to say about this subject from the same book we read from earlier.

> *Successful people only have two problems dealing with negative feedback. However, they are big problems: (a) they don't want to hear it from us and (b) we don't want to give it to them.*[26]

Marshall goes on to explain all the reasons why it is so difficult to give negative feedback to successful people like you. Yes, like you. See if you can tell what the underlying problem is. Hint: We discussed this earlier.

> *It's not hard to see why people don't want to hear negative feedback. Successful people are incredibly delusional about their achievements. Over 95 percent of the members in most successful groups believe that they perform in the top half of their group. While this is statistically ridiculous, it is psychologically real.*[27]

What makes successful people delusional about their capabilities? Did I hear the word "ego"? Yes. An uncontrolled ego is the killer of all things humble. It destroys our ability to be servant leaders, Level 5 leaders, inspirational leaders, and any other model you would want to emulate. It basically destroys your ability to lead.

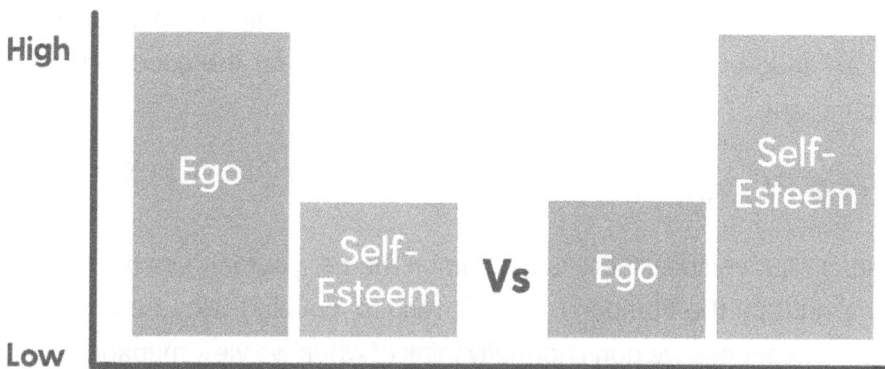

---

26 Goldsmith, *What Got You Here Won't Get You There,* 111.
27 Goldsmith, *What Got You Here Won't Get You There,* 111.

Draw a seesaw in your mind's eye. Self-esteem on one end, ego on the other. Raise your self-esteem, your ego drops. You still have an ego, and that is good, because you need it. Just like body fat. The idea is not to get rid of all body fat. That leads to death. But so does too much of it. Too much ego will destroy your leadership career.

To my point, Marshall continues:

> *Feedback generally doesn't break through to successful people even when we adopt the eminently sane guideline of depersonalizing the feedback. That is, talk about the task, not the person. This is easy in theory. But successful people's identities are often so closely connected to what they do that it's naïve to assume they will not take it personally when receiving negative feedback about the most important activity in their lives.*
>
> *Basically, we accept feedback that is consistent with our self-image and reject feedback that is inconsistent.*[28]

Personally, I believe that Marshall is overstating the case here. I don't experience leaders being quite as defensive to feedback as he suggests. However, I do think he makes a good point: people's identities are often wrapped up in their work.

Taking a quick rabbit trail, let me say that my hope for you is that you can both be a Level 5 leader (very humble and very driven) and not make the mistake of seeing your work as what defines you. My friend, you are so much more than a human doing. You're a human being. And there is more to life than work. If your work is your life, your life work will be less than fulfilling as you reflect back over the years. You need to have a personal life too. OK. I am getting off my soapbox.

---

28 Goldsmith, *What Got You Here Won't Get You There*, 112.

Back to Marshall:

> *I have other issues with traditional face-to-face negative feedback—and almost all of them boil down to the fact that it focuses on the past (a failed past at that), not a positive future.*[29]

Wow. If you take all that to heart, no wonder you are not getting much constructive feedback from your leader! And here is some useful information: the higher up the food chain you go in leadership, the less feedback you receive. Some of what you just read explains it.

There are also other reasons, like:

1. You are expected to be excellent at what you do, so you don't get positive feedback for being excellent.

2. When you stop being excellent, your employer will get someone else. See #1.

3. You are likely to get defensive when getting negative feedback, so your less-than-excellent areas will be tolerated because of all the great work you do in other areas. When you dip below a certain threshold, your employer will get someone else.

You are likely asking yourself, "Why not just give some advance feedback to help this person see that they have areas in which they need to improve?" The analogy I use to explain this phenomenon is a black peppercorn in your teeth. Have you ever gone to lunch with a friend and had something like a dang peppercorn get stuck in between two front teeth?

I am cringing as I write this. You go the whole lunch laughing and smiling from ear to ear, looking like an idiot, and your friend says n-o-t-h-i-n-g!

---

29 Goldsmith, *What Got You Here Won't Get You There*, 112.

After lunch, in the restroom, you see a cringe-worthy sight and wonder why your friend did not say a word. Some of you are saying, "I speak up. I tell them to go get it." Good for you, but you are in the minority. Most are hesitant to embarrass you by telling you how awful you look. So, they let it go.

We live in a polite society, and it takes a lot of courage and a big emotional investment in the relationship to try to help someone see negative areas of their performance that may be sensitive.

All that to say that getting feedback is difficult **but** necessary for you to grow.

The good news is that you can take a surefire approach that is guaranteed to get you the constructive feedback you need to better serve your customers, north, south, east, and west. I call it the MLS technique.

More of, Less of, Same of (MLS)

In order to get quality feedback from any vector, you need to ask. That requires sublimating your ego much of the time and admitting that you don't have all the answers.

Here are the scripts you can use with each vector.

This is a chapter on the western vector, so we will start there.

MLS West

Say this to your colleague in another department:

In order to help me and my people do a better job of working with you and your team, let's use the SOLID MLS technique.

It works like this: we will take turns answering a series of three questions, going back and forth until we are done.

1. In order for me to (serve you better) (partner better) (collaborate better) (communicate better), what can I do <u>more of</u> to be more helpful?

2. In order for me to … (same), what can my team and I do <u>less of</u> to be more helpful?

3. In order for me to … (same), what can I do the <u>same of</u>?

MLS South

Say this to your direct reports in a one-on-one: I want to be a better leader for you. I want to go through a series of three questions that will help me understand how I can do so.

1. In order for me to manage and lead you more effectively, what can I do more of?

2. Less of?

3. What should I continue doing the same of?

MLS East

Say this to your external customer:

I want to better partner with you to help us work better together and to be easier to work with. What can we do:

1. More of, to better serve you?

2. Less of, to better serve you?

3. The same of, to continue to serve you?

MLS North

Say this to your leader:

I want to improve my work for you and the organization, and I need your help. Can I ask you a few questions and will you please be completely candid with me? I promise not to get defensive.

1. What can I do more of, to be the best leader on your team?

2. What can I do less of, to be the best leader?

3. What should I continue doing the same way?

The Key to Keeping the Feedback Coming

In order to keep the lines of communication open in any vector, you need to avoid getting defensive and resist the temptation to give context to try to change your feedback source's opinion. Otherwise, it will be the last time you get truly candid feedback.

You can think of MLS as "feedforward" because it is actionable. Instead of dealing with what you are not doing right, focus on these three areas:

1. More of …

2. Less of …

3. Same of …

Take Action

Once you get this valuable feedback, take action. Address the issues that were brought up, and then circle back to your feedback source for checkpoints to gauge if you are making progress. Remember. Do not get defensive or give excuses. Simply say, "Thank you for the input. I appreciate it. What else?"

Doing this is guaranteed to lower your ego, create more humility, give you invaluable, actionable insight, and make you a better leader.

Breaking Down Silos

As we wrap up this chapter, we would do our discussion a great disservice if we left organizational silos unaddressed. Let's bring back Patrick Lencioni, one of my favorite authors, who wrote a great book on how to break down silos.

> *Silos are nothing more than the barriers that exist between departments within an organization, causing people who are supposed to be on the same team to work against one another. And whether we call this phenomenon departmental politics, divisional rivalry, or turf warfare, it is one of the frustrating aspects of life in any sizable organization.[30]*

If you are the CEO, know that you are the one best suited to break down the silos in your company. Departmental executives need you to help. They cannot effectively do it without you.

If you are an executive who reports to a CEO, besides getting your CEO to read this, you can do a lot to help break down silos. It will require you partnering with your western colleagues in a big way. It will also require you "leading up."

> *Even the most well-meaning, intelligent people get distracted and confused amid the endless list of tactical and administrative details that come their way every day. Pulled in many directions without a compass, they pursue seemingly worthwhile agendas under the assumption that their efforts will be in the best interest of the organization as a whole.[31]*

I am sure you feel like this at times. Notice the "pulled in many directions without a compass" comment. Thank you, Patrick!

---

30 Patrick Lencioni, *Silos, Politics, and Turf Wars* (San Francisco: Jossey-Bass, 2006), 175-176.

31 Lencioni, *Silos, Politics, and Turf Wars*, 176.

He goes on to write:

> *But as employees notice their colleagues in other divisions repeatedly moving in different directions, they begin to wonder why they aren't on board. Over time, their confusion turns into disappointment, which eventually becomes resentment—even hostility—toward their supposed teammates. And then the worst thing happens— they actually start working against those colleagues on purpose!* [32]

Does any part of this describe your organization? If so, remember the section earlier where we talked about you "leading up"? This is a prime example of what you need to do. Influence your CEO to get involved in fixing this problem, to whatever degree it exists.

> *If there is a place where the blame for silos and politics belongs, it is at the top of an organization. Every departmental silo in any company can ultimately be traced back to the leaders of those departments, who have failed to understand the interdependencies that must exist among the executive team, or who have failed to make those interdependencies clear to the people deeper in their own departments.* [33]

Here is how it can be done. Patrick gives us the solution:

> *Thankfully, there is a simple and powerful way for those leaders to create a common sense of purpose, and a context for interdependency: they must establish, for the executive team as well as the rest of the organization, a rallying cry. A thematic goal.* [34]

---

32 Lencioni, *Silos, Politics, and Turf Wars*, 176.
33 Lencioni, *Silos, Politics, and Turf Wars*, 177.
34 Lencioni, *Silos, Politics, and Turf Wars*, 177.

To break down silos, you need to make it crystal clear to everyone exactly what the priorities are. And there needs to be an even clearer MAIN priority.

What is your main focus for this year or this quarter?

What is your rallying cry?

For Further Discussion

- As you look west, where are your most challenging relationships?

- How have you tried to improve these relationships?

- What worked? What didn't?

- As a result of reading this section, what actions can and will you take to improve your level of customer service to your western colleagues?

CHAPTER 5

YOUR RALLYING CRY

Chapter 5: **YOUR RALLYING CRY**

In the foreword, you read the email I received from Bharath. He said, " 'Protect Our Plan' was a resounding success!" What did he mean? Allow me to interpret.

Rallying Cries Work

Bharath meant that the Service Delivery organization was highly successful in achieving the 2020 plan of delivered revenue. "Protect Our Plan" was the rallying cry for the year. In Patrick Lencioni's vernacular, that slogan was the thematic goal. Everyone in the Service Delivery organization got on board with this focus.

In fact, we passed around a basketball, and the entire extended leadership team signed the ball autograph-style, saying "Yes, I am on board with the plan." That ball has sat on Bharath's desk all year. It symbolically said, "Yes, we will protect delivered revenue. Yes, we will achieve our goal. Yes, everyone will get their bonuses!" And so, they did. Again, congratulations to this team!

Now, I have the privilege of once again facilitating an offsite. Once again, we will be developing a rallying cry. What will it be this year? Will it cause people to get motivated and spring into action? It is going to be a tough act to follow, because they did so well last year.

I do know this year we will be signing a soccer ball.

Building on a Previous Rallying Cry

In order to tie together 2020 with 2021, we have decided to keep the first part of the rallying cry. So, it will be "Protect Our Plan and ..." something. I don't know what. But it will be organic, coming

from these forty top leaders as they coalesce around a thematic goal for 2021.

Will this book, *Your Customer Compass*, influence their thinking? I hope so. Bharath really wants the east-west highway addressed in a big way. As I was going over my ideas for this customer compass model, he really thought that the main areas of need were right there. I agree.

Each organization will have a customer corridor that they need to work on.

What is yours?

Other Vectors

As we leave this chapter, I want to acknowledge that what we have not explored are some of the concepts like west-north and south-east relationships. There is plenty of room left for more chapters of this book in a revised edition! For now, we both have our work cut out for us. You have to determine which corridor needs the most work, and what to do about it. I have to go prepare for an offsite!

CHAPTER 6

CONCLUSION

Chapter 6: CONCLUSION

Using Your Compass

There is no substitute for experience. In order to get really good at serving your stakeholders, north, south, east, and west, you have to practice. The good news is that you will have plenty of opportunities. As you strive for improvement in serving these vectors, you will get input along the way if you are open to it, and if you ask.

Just like there is no substitute for experience, there is no substitute for asking for help. Doing so will humble you, and that is a good thing. We all need that. Me more than most. So, ask others for help. Ask for input into how you are doing with those people who are particularly difficult customers.

Navigation for the Journey

The more you use your compass, the easier it will become to navigate the myriad of customer relationships you have. And the more you will enjoy the journey. Now, you can look at your heading and make course corrections based on your successes or failures in delivering great customer service to each vector.

Hopefully, you also can better align or orient your position on the company map to those around you, 360 degrees, as you also have a better bearing of who is your customer.

A Great Reading List

You have been presented with much wisdom here by my extensive quoting of some very well-known and highly reputable thinkers. These are proven practices that are guaranteed to work, if you will work them. They are also guaranteed not to work if you don't.

I trust that you are already working most of them. My hope is that you gleaned a few good ideas that will help you be even better as you lead your organization.

Please note the bibliography. This would be a great reading list for any leader wanting to grow their skills and abilities.

Age-Old Wisdom

The truths contained in this short little book are not my own. They are age-old wisdom from the best leaders on the planet. I have not had an original thought. All that I have given you has come from these amazing leaders who have allowed me to pick up their trade secrets and pass them along to leaders like you.

Thank you for the privilege of speaking into your life for the past few hours. I sincerely wish you much continued success.

Multiply Yourself

As a leader, you are influential in your world. I encourage you to take the information contained in these pages and disseminate them to your customers. All of them. North. South. East. West.

May you continue to lead well, and may you have great joy in your work and in your life. Let the journey continue!

For Further Discussion

- What are some practical applications of this compass model that you can immediately put to good use?

- Which of the four quadrants is your weakest?

- What actions are you going to take to address that issue?

- Which corridor is your weakest? North-south or east-west? What will you do about it?

About the Author

Daniel J. Mueller

Managing Director

SOLIDleaders, LLC

SOLIDleaders.com

Cell: 832.732.9395

Daniel@solidleaders.com

www.LinkedIn.com/in/
SOLIDleaders/

Executive Coaching Specializations

Executive Leadership Coaching

(Growing to the Next Level)

Executive Career Coaching

(Getting a New Executive Job)

Onboarding Coaching

(Starting a New Executive Job)

Portfolio Life Coaching

(Moving into Semi-retirement)

High Potential Coaching

(Emerging Future Leaders)

Executive Team Coaching

(All-Hands Team Coaching)

Practice Development

(Coach-the-Coach for Internal or
Professional Coaches)

Daniel Mueller is one of the earliest and most active pioneers of the executive coaching industry. As of 2020, he has provided executive coaching for more than 1,525 CEOs and executives, delivered 50,000+ hours of one-on-one executive coaching, and been privileged to witness major transformation in the lives of most clients.

Passionate about serving leaders at every level, Daniel is dedicated to helping executives become more effective in all aspects of their personal and professional lives. Prior to specializing in executive coaching, he was CEO of a management training company, a business advisory firm, and an organizational development consultancy—all three of which heavily influenced his unique approach to executive coaching.

In addition to drawing on these disciplines, Daniel has extensive training in the behavioral sciences, behavioral psychology, and executive career counseling. An avid student of executive leadership, he regularly speaks and publishes on subjects critical to executive peak performance.

Since 1996, Daniel has specialized in CEO and executive coaching, working in three main areas: leadership coaching, helping executives remove blind spots, leverage strengths, and overcome weaknesses; executive career coaching, helping executives transition from one role to another; and executive onboarding coaching, helping executives start new roles. He also provides training for professional leadership, career, and life coaches, and has a sub-specialty and passion around coaching faith-based leaders of non-profits.

Since his first executive coaching engagement in 1987, Daniel knew he had found his calling, and had a meteoric rise to the top of the emerging executive coaching profession. However, the more outwardly successful Daniel became, the greater the internal pain grew of feeling like an imposter. He chose to numb this pain with alcohol, which led him into recovery for alcoholism—his sobriety date is March 4, 1996. Humbled and broken, Daniel began diligently working to attain personal transformation. This story of amazing success, total failure, and complete redemption has led to one of his favorite sayings: "I coach from a place of weakness, not strength." From the wreckage emerged a tried-and-true methodology for helping any executive grow to the next level—if they are willing to do what it takes. Daniel is a good example of, "If he can do it, anyone can."

From 1990 to 1996, Daniel served as President and CEO of Solid Foundation International Inc., an organizational design and development consultancy. There, he led team-building initiatives, administered hundreds of interview-based 360° assessments for executive coaching clients, and created individualized leadership development plans.

From 1986 to 1990, Daniel was CEO of MAI, a management consultancy acquired in 1990 by Organizational Leadership and Development, Inc., and from 1982 to 1986, he was CEO of Wellness Consultants, Inc., a management training company. He began his career in 1975 as a personal trainer and fitness coach.

Daniel started college at the State University of New York at Stony Brook and relocated to Austin to complete a degree in the Plan 2 Honors Program in Liberal Arts at the University of Texas at Austin, which he never finished. He is gratefully married to the love of his life, Patty, and has three awesome daughters.

About SOLIDleaders

SOLIDleaders, LLC is an innovative global leader and trusted advisor delivering business and personal transformation to senior leaders.

Our team of seasoned CEOs and senior executives are skilled change agents whose proven success helps organizations and their leaders achieve measurable results. Our broad industry experience supports companies from startups to the Fortune 500.

SOLIDleaders' purpose is to transform leaders, those whom they lead, and the organizations they run, delivering superior, leading-edge CEO and board advising, senior executive coaching, and C-suite consulting with quantifiable return on investment.

Bibliography

Block, Peter. *Stewardship: Choosing Service Over Self-Interest*. San Francisco: Berrett-Koehler Publishers, Inc., 1993.

Bradberry, Travis and Jean Greaves. *Emotional Intelligence 2.0*. San Diego: TalentSmart, 2009.

Branden, Nathaniel. *Self-Esteem at Work: How Confident People Make Powerful Companies*. San Francisco: Jossey-Bass, 1998.

Bryant, Adam. "For This Guru, No Question Is Too Big." *New York Times*, May 23, 2009. *https://www.nytimes.com/2009/05/24/business/24collins.html*.

Collins, Jim. *Good to Great: Why Some Companies Make the Leap… and Others Don't*. New York: HarperCollins, 2001.

Covey, Stephen M. R. *The Speed of Trust: The One Thing That Changes Everything*. New York: Free Press, 2006.

Freiberg, Kevin L., and Jacquelyn A. Freiberg. *Nuts! Southwest Airlines' Crazy Recipe for Business and Personal Success*. New York: Bard Books, 1996.

Goldsmith, Marshall. *What Got You Here Won't Get You There: How Successful People Become Even More Successful*. New York: Hachette Books, 2014.

Griffin, Jill. *Customer Loyalty: How to Earn It, How to Keep It*. New York: Lexington Books, 1995.

Holiday, Ryan. *Ego is the Enemy*. New York: Portfolio / Penguin, 2016.

Lencioni, Patrick. *Silos, Politics, and Turf Wars*. San Francisco: Jossey-Bass, 2006.

Lencioni, Patrick. *The Advantage: Why Organizational Health Trumps Everything Else in Business*. San Francisco: Jossey-Bass, 2012.

Publishers Weekly. "Nonfiction Book Review: GOOD TO GREAT: Why Some Companies Make the Leap... And Others Don't." Last modified September 3, 2001. *https://www.publishersweekly.com/978-0-06-662099-2*.

Trammell, Joel. *The CEO Tightrope: How to Master the Balancing Act of a Successful CEO*. Austin, Texas: Greenleaf Book Group Press, 2014.

Wickman, Gino. *Traction: Get a Grip on Your Business*. Dallas, TX: BenBella Books, Inc., 2011.

Wikimedia Foundation, Inc. "Good to Great." Wikipedia. Last modified October 29, 2020. *https://en.wikipedia.org/wiki/Good_to_Great*.

Wikimedia Foundation, Inc. "Peter Principle." Wikipedia. Last modified February 5, 2021. *https://en.wikipedia.org/wiki/Peter_principle*.

Wikimedia Foundation, Inc. "Servant leadership." Wikipedia. Last modified January 23, 2021. *https://en.wikipedia.org/wiki/Servant_leadership*.

Appendix

Dan Rourke Case Study

Dan Rourke started as Director of Customer Support for Cadence Design Systems (NASDAQ: CDNS) in June 1998. Prior to this, Dan had a nineteen-year career at IBM, with his last position as Global Offerings Executive.

At Cadence, Dan was a junior executive who was producing results consistent with high potentials. He had been promoted to Group Director in April of 2001 and needed to continue his growth and development at this new level. Pat McCarty, then Vice President of North America Customer Support, had eleven direct reports, and did not have as much time to invest in growing Dan as she would have liked. Also, she wanted to have an outside, objective third party identify Dan's true potential. She was developing a succession plan and wanted to find the few executives who belonged on her shortlist. Pat saw executive coaching as an excellent vehicle to provide the direct intentional development of Dan that was needed to augment her existing mentorship.

In October 2001, Dan and I began coaching under a Cadence contract. We completed a 360, and Dan willingly shared the results with Pat. Several key issues were identified. It was generally agreed that if Dan could grow past these, he would be in the running to succeed Pat when she advanced her career. As a result of the coaching, Dan was more intentional in his assessment of Pat, asking for her mentorship and determining which key areas she wanted to see addressed in order for Dan to demonstrate next-level capability.

The 360-degree assessment revealed a significant number of Dan's positive attributes. Sue, a participant in the assessment, captured much of the essence of the strengths portion of Dan's feedback. "Dan has strong organizing ability, he is open to ideas, responsive, able to quickly grasp new ideas and respond to them. I am also impressed with his ability to take suggestions for improvement to heart. Another of Dan's top strengths is analysis and synthesis, particularly as it relates to processes. Further, Dan has very strong project management instincts and abilities. And last but most importantly, Dan is a man of integrity. You can always count on him to be above reproach when it comes to honesty, keeping his word, treating employees fairly, adhering to company policy, and demonstrating strong business ethics."

Neil's feedback echoed Sue's comments, with some additional strengths. "Dan has strategic insight, in particular, his ability to see the consequences of decisions on our future. Dan is also a very strong communicator, and does a great job delivering messages, and responding to tough questions with a measured response."

Another employee, Susan, added two more strengths representative of the feedback from the twenty participants I interviewed during this qualitative 360. Susan said, "I see Dan as a strong leader. I see him lead and I see others want to follow him. Also, he finds time to develop his direct reports, he makes time to coach, and develop careers, and generally keep abreast of everyone's top issues. Further, Dan encourages work-life balance, and walks the talk in this area."

The major weaknesses that Dan and I identified were his cross-functional and upward-facing relationships and his reticence to be more of a leader throughout the organization. He tended to focus on his direct organization, which ran like clockwork, was not spending time with other areas, and was unsure how to go to the next level as a leader.

Over the course of the next year, actions were taken to address these weaknesses. An action I recommended he take on November 28th, 2001 is telling: "Discuss the process of promotion to VP with Pat and gain insight into key relationships needed; design a one-page action plan with a timeline leading to an October 2002 promotion." At that same time, I emailed Dan a booklet I had published, *SOLID Goal Setting for Leaders*, which caused him to set goals in every area of his life, and which he found transformational. Dan set very clear goals and achieved those goals by working on peer and cross-functional relationship building, driving consensus, gaining buy-in, and leading collaboration on problem-solving. We worked on a weekly basis to identify peer and superior relationships that he needed to build, and strategies for becoming a more influential leader.

Dan succeeded Pat McCarty as head of the global support team in February of 2005 and was promoted to Vice President of Global Customer Support in April of 2006. He was recognized with the newly created Cadence Outstanding Leadership award on January 29th, 2008 and continues to grow in significance as a work and community leader. He attributes much of his success to the executive coaching we did. He says, "The immediate focus of our coaching was on the needs I had to expand my influence and develop better external relationships. However, the principles I learned through the coaching have been applicable across many situations and growth opportunities since then. I have also been able to use many of the same techniques and approaches to mentor and coach high-potential members of my team to higher performance."

www.ingramcontent.com/pod-product-compliance
Lightning Source LLC
Chambersburg PA
CBHW050510210326
41521CB00011B/2403